The Architecture of Control

A Contribution to the Critique of the Science of Apparatuses

The Architecture of Control

A Contribution to the Critique of the Science of Apparatuses

Grant Vetter

Winchester, UK
Washington, USA

First published by Zero Books, 2012
Zero Books is an imprint of John Hunt Publishing Ltd., Laurel House, Station Approach,
Alresford, Hants, SO24 9JH, UK
office1@jhpbooks.net
www.johnhuntpublishing.com
www.zero-books.net

For distributor details and how to order please visit the 'Ordering' section on our website.

Text copyright: Grant Vetter 2012

ISBN: 978 1 78099 293 8

A CIP catalogue record for this book is available from the British Library.

Design: Stuart Davies

Printed and bound by CPI Group (UK) Ltd, Croydon, CR0 4YY

We operate a distinctive and ethical publishing philosophy in all
areas of our business, from our global network of authors to
production and worldwide distribution.

CONTENTS

Dedicated to Wendy and Katie.

If the capitalist market and the 'inspection house' (the plan) are two forms of the same thing, and this thing, as I will show, is ultimately a disciplinary mechanism in which the individuals' freedom is limited to a choice from a given menu and they are prevented from defining the *context* of their interaction, then emancipatory political theory and practice must find a way beyond this dichotomy, to discover forms of social interaction that cannot be reduced to the disciplinary and organizational features of the market or the prison.[1]

Massimo De Angelis

Acknowledgements

First and foremost, I would like to thank Katie Herzog, both for the homage my book pays to the title of one of her artist-book projects — *Feng Shuing the Panopticon* — and for her practice as an artist, which has been both inspiring and timely. Her ability to develop dynamic forms of artistic and social practice that are situated at the site of knowledge production has certainly been an invaluable contribution to the project undertaken here. In locating and comparing conceptual incongruities through experimental lexicongraphy, new methods of disjunctive librarianship and alternative models of archivization, her work opens up new spaces for thinking about epistemology and power in the discursive field — a theme which figures prominently throughout this text. Such an endeavor is certainly one of the most pressing issues of our day, both creating a potential for what Foucault called the 'unthought' as well as a confrontation with the categorical determinations of bio-power and governmentality. Above all else, it is Herzog's rigorous questioning of textual and aesthetic categories that this text finds a certain shared trajectory with — as well as the hope of resisting (neo)Panopticism. These constants in Herzog's work have been a wonderful lesson for me in reflecting not only on the abstract qualities of language, but on the concrete interventions that can be made in language as a thing, a texture, a template and a tempest of imaginative potentials. Our exchanges have always been furtive ones and I encourage all the readers of this work to investigate her publications as well as her curatorial and artistic projects as they have been a guiding light in the production of this work.

I would also like to thank Justin Bower for the feedback and regular criticism I receive from him regarding many of the 'live' debates around post-humanism and subjectivation. His regular

I

countenance shows itself throughout these pages in any number of unexpected ways. Bower's work as a cultural producer provides a visual counterpart to many of the theories of social control that appear in the pages of this text as well as highlighting some of the conflicted genealogies herein. Through very different mediums we have both been engaged in struggling to define the notion of a 'weak' or 'saturated' subject in various ways for some time now and this text purports to be just one more contribution to that ongoing conversation.

I also own a very special debt of gratitude to Alain Badiou whose personal encouragement and valorization of the manifesto form provided me with a set of permissions to follow my own political commitments and aesthetic inclinations. His spirited defense of philosophy in recent years shows itself in the pages that follow in innumerable ways and has been essential to both the themes and content of this work. His reflections on subjectivation are, perhaps, the most incisive interventions since Lacan or Althusser, and they also play a defining role in the arguments undertaken here.

The advice of Wolfgang Schirmacher also shows itself throughout this work in any number of ways, especially in the sections that address Heidegger, the question of being and the end of metaphysics. My gratitude for his contribution is of the highest measure. He has been an influential figure on the scene of continental philosophy for some time now and his work on culture and technology has motivated a great number of the insights in this text. My heartfelt thanks are extended not only for his personal guidance and mentorship but also for his endless encouragement and boundless enthusiasm for the philosophical enterprise.

This short book also owes a great debt as well to my graduate and undergraduate students at the School of Science and Architecture in California who continue to challenge me with provocative questions about the practice of architecture and its relationship to subjectivation. There is perhaps no better stimulus to continue to delve deeper into the research archives than the exchange of ideas engendered by classroom discussions. I will always be incredibly thankful for the time and care my students have taken in helping to educate me about specific issues pertaining to the relationship of practice and theory, and for making a spirited debate around architecture a regular part of my congress.

In addition to these very personal relationships this work also sits upon the accomplishments of a number of contemporary Foucaultians and theorists in the burgeoning field of surveillance studies, many of whom appear in my endnotes but who should also be mentioned here: Didier Bido, Willam Bogard, Massimo De Angelis, Gary Genosko, Kevin G. Haggerty, Maria Los, David Lyon, Toshimaru Ogura and Mark Poster. Beyond the work of these scholars this text is marked, inscribed upon, negotiated and permeated throughout by all the professors who have had a profound influence on how I think about the notion of subjectivation. They are, in no particular order, Giorgio Agamben, Judith Butler, Juli Carson, Simon Critchley, Manual Delanda, Michael Hardt, Daniel Joseph Martinez, Brian Massumi, Avital Ronell, Wolfgang Schirmacher, Andrezej J. Warminski, and Slavoj Žižek. Last but not least, this text was allowed to come to fruition through the loving generosity of my wife and family who have always encouraged my passion for philosophy.

Prolegomenon to Six Meditations on the Architecture of Subjectivation

A society is thus composed of certain foregrounded practices organizing its normative institutions *and* of innumerable other practices that remain "minor", always there but not organizing discourse and preserving the beginnings or remains of different (institutional, scientific) hypothesis for that society of others. It is in this multifarious and silent "reserve" of producers that we should look for "consumer" practices having the double character pointed out by Foucault, of being able to organize both spaces and languages, whether on a minute or a vast scale.[2]

Michel de Certeau

Far from preventing knowledge, power produces it.[3]

Michel Foucault

In as much as feng shui may be at odds with conventional religion and morality, it also challenges our conception of knowledge.[4]

Ole Brunn

0.1 Techniques of Archio-Discipline: Panopticism and Fend Shui.

It's somewhat peculiar that Panopticism and Feng Shui, the two great populace discourses on architecture and social control, haven't been thought of as conversant topos on the micro-physics of architectural power. But why is this? Of course, there is the eastern/western divide and the fact that one of these systems of belief predates the other by more than a millennium. However, the obvious answer to the question at hand is that the first of these two dispositif's is only a 'populace' discourse in academia,

4

and the field of surveillance studies in particular, while the second has become a massified discourse about neo-spiritualist design strategies.[5] As such, we can say that they are not populace discourses in exactly the same sense. Panopticism is a model of architectural discipline — or as Foucault would have it, a system of techniques associated with the development of self-regulating power[6] — while Feng Shui is based on how orientations, energy flows and material objects effect our sense of psychological well-being, (or at least, this is the westernized notion of Feng Shui practices).[7]

0.2 Universalized Panopticism: Underdetermination and Overdetermination as Models of Social Control.

Paradoxically, it is this marked difference between high and low motifs — between strong architectural interpellation and weak orientational determinism — that makes the dialog between Panopticism and Feng Shui a site of critical import. Not only is the heterogeneity of these two disciplines a means of deconstructing the binary oppositions of rationalism/mysticism, design/divination, functionalism/taboo, control of the visible field/control of the ancestral past, etc., — but the twofold deployment of these diagrams of control in the home, the workplace, the classroom, the hospital and almost every other architectural apparatus is a sign that we have come to live in a time of universalized Panopticism. This appears to be the case not only because hyper-Panoptic surveillance is spreading through every 'developed' and developing nation, but also because Feng Shui techniques often disrupt the deployment of Panoptic power — offering us something of a positive reaction-formation to the hegemonic forms of social control that condition the body socius today.[8]

0.3 On the (re)Distribution of Architectural Discipline: Rational, Spiritual and Aesthetic.

While Panopticism enjoys a broad equality of distribution in relation to security measures, workplace monitoring and even scopophelic forms of entertainment, the rapidly expanding field of Feng Shui practices still seems to represent an esoteric ecology of exchanges in the popular mind. Evolving out of disparate rural beliefs and mystic traditions, Feng Shui has been re-appropriated by western models of functionalism in order to be repackaged and sold to fortune five hundred companies, specialized interior design firms and a fledgling industry of pseudo-spiritual advisors. As such, Feng Shui can be characterized as a duplicitous discipline that promotes a sense of architectural control, (or control over architecture), by attributing a supra-natural dimension to the arrangement of objects.[9]

However, beyond the reification and/or popularization of its practices, what has given Feng Shui a new sense of purchase in the present is how its varied methodologies work to undermine the unlimited extension of Panoptic determinations and archio-disciplinary measures. Among its highly specialized schools, anti-Panoptic techniques of arrangement and distribution are central concerns without being interpreted as part of an explicit political agenda. Instead, such counter-statist positions are associated with redirecting qi (energy flow) into a balanced relationship with the surrounding environment — reasserting a sense of harmony over the composition of lived space as well as against the designs of well-controlled space. Considered from this point of view, Panopticism seems to be a mode of architectural interpolation that is everywhere aligned with the directives of governmentality, while Feng Shui appears to be closer to neo-spiritual, aesthetic, and even quasi-humanist concerns.[10]

0.4 Challenging the Micro-physics of Power from East to West: Popular and Critical Genealogies of Self-Mastery.

In light of this conflicted state of affairs, we should attempt to ask a rather pedestrian question, or at least, a seemingly obvious one: could the critical use of Feng Shui be one of the answers Foucault was searching for in valorizing 'techniques of the self' as a mode of resistance to Panoptic domination?[11] And might the different readings of architectural power offered up by practitioners of Feng Shui be a crucial consideration in attempting to locate counter-Enlightenment strategies to the omnipresence of networked Panopticism? At the very least, isn't the sudden spread and westernization of Feng Shui practices the populist answer to the naturalization of Panoptic systems of control — despite how conflicted, contradictory and commercial such motivations might seem? In short, can Feng Shui, with its many schools and historical permutations, offer us a place to think about the conditions of subjective freedom in relation to societies of control and techno-Panoptic surveillance?

0.5 Architecture and Askesis: Practices of Revolutionary Domesticity.

Lest such an inquiry be mistaken for being too casual or even ironic, we should also consider whether it is merely coincidental that Foucault's time at Berkeley coincided with the explosion of Feng Shui studies at that same institution — and whether or not there are traces of this influence in Foucault's texts — even traces which appear struck through, under erasure or in abeyance.[12] It might be more radical still to go looking for evidence of Feng Shui in Foucault's own living arrangements — in the intimate archipelago of the domicile and the archives of domestic habitation.

Whether these answers are sought in Foucault's texts or homes, or even the intertextual localities that permeate his oeuvre, the omission of eastern models of design from Foucault's varied genealogies of power continue to be a pressing issue for architectural scholarship today. Looking into this missing file in Foucault's archeological dossier might allow us to rethink the deployment of Panoptic power under terms which are diametrically opposed to both rationalist (modern) and anti-rationalist (postmodern) models of organizing space. Engaging with new approaches to the question of Panopticism might also provide us with a different notion of self-mastery, (or what Foucault called pre-Christian practices of askesis), that would unhinge the determinations of disciplinary environments and/or the carceral eye of power.[13]

0.6 Rethinking Feng Shui: Geomantic Divination as a Form of Interstitial Materialism.

Alongside these initial concerns we might also want to consider the various schools of Feng Shui to be something like an eccentric agglomeration of discourses that actively engage with marginalized sites of power in the Panoptic order — such as the home, the apartment and contemplative arrangements of the landscape, cityscape and rural environs.

Or, it could be equally fortuitous to look at the discipline of Feng Shui as an art of addressing interstitial spaces — as being something like the micro-management of an *inter-relational aesthetics* between town and county, home and community, neighbor and neighbor, room and furniture, ancestor and descendent, etc. From such a vantage point, the conditions of in-betweeness addressed by Feng Shui are implicated in adjudicating the connections that link (1) city planning and agricultural organization, (2) architectural design and sociality, and (3) the mode of production and metaphysical functionalism, i.e., of being an archio-spiritual science based on understanding how architectonic forms fortify or unsettle the field of social relations.

Or, looked at through the rubric of historical materialism, the different schools of Feng Shui could be thought of as a means of re-distributing architectural space in relation to the organization of base and superstructure, i.e., of addressing daily needs and the (pre)conditions of their structural fulfillment. Such a revaluation of Feng Shui practices could give rise to an entirely different notion of socio-political enculturation with regard to infra- and superstructural concerns — or simply a different (political) economy of means, distributions and partitions.

Last but not least, it could prove equally advantageous to go even further back in time and reconsider the ancient tradition of Feng Shui as a means of addressing the pre-*sent* — but this kind of analogical comparison would mean recasting geomantic divination under the sign of geometric metaphysics, or even as a system of geometric micro-physics, i.e., of spiritualized practices that address the Panoptic imaginary through strategic determinations of orientation and alignment. Perhaps contemporary forms of Feng Shui might even be seen as a stand-in, and in some instances, as a counterbalance to the types of self-reflexive architectural relations that Foucault addressed under the Benthamian theme of 'soul training' — even if posited in a somewhat oblique and removed manner.[14] Irrespective of which of these trajectories is the most plausible, (or at least the most furtive), Feng Shui remains the site of a certain potenza in the field of architectural praxis that stands at the intersection of historical, political and aesthetic concerns as well as providing a challenge to how we think about inter-subjective relations, the stratification/territorialization of the body socius and the process of subjectivation.

0.7 Power/Knowledge and Surveillance: On the Question of 'Dwelling' in a Worldwide Panopticon.

Such a long series of questions is itself circumscribed by relations of Power/Knowledge vis-à-vis the legitimation of institutional and commercial discourses; the defense of western rationalism and eastern mysticism; the proliferation of systems of training, certification and patronage in architectural education and geomantic divination; the propagation of judico-legal permissions for individual and state sanctioned architectural practices; the endless production and reproduction of ancient proviso's and modern engineering standards, etc. As a consequence of these nefarious forms of interpolation, there is no longer a localizable outside to the world of judico-archio-disciplinary relations. Contrary to the Heideggerian hope of developing authentic modes of dwelling, being-in-the-world has become synonymous with being enmeshed in a panoply of architectural diagrams where concerns about shelter and building are just the particularities of existing in a worldwide Panopticon that extends from Google earth and satellite spectrography to eye-in-the-sky drones and an ever expanding catalog of ground surveillance.[15] Universalized Panopticism is now deployed in parallel measure across the dense topologies of slums and the wide-open spaces of gated communities — where the intra-subjective effects of Panoptic/penal life are internalized by rich and poor alike.

This transformation of public and private space, or really their collapse into one another, is what makes any simple dichotomy between Feng Shui practices and Panopticism increasing obsolete. Every determination of eastern intuition and western belief, rationalism and mysticism, religious authority and pragmatic regulation, must now be thought of as coextensive, mutually determined and even structurally overdetermined. In an unexpected turn of events, techno-Panopticism has concretized a metaphysical dimension of power that Feng Shui practices only ever hypothesized (omnipresence), while Feng Shui has become commercially successful in a way that continues to elude the rationalist dictation of spatial arrangements. As an unexpected correlative, disciplinary architecture takes on a mystical dimension that needs to be resisted, while mysticism becomes a necessary qualifier for the defense of geomantic divination — but only because both are circumscribed by an electro-magnetic field of power that deals with the simultaneity of past, present and future action — surveilled or otherwise.

0.8 The (sub)Divided Gaze of Neo-Panoptic Power: Hyper-Interpellation and the Birth of the Observational-Industrial-Complex.

Under this new set of conditions, we find ourselves born into the architectural/observational gaze of power; its conscious and unconscious presuppositions; its normalizing and reifying strictures; its devoted symbols and scripted spaces.[16] But in comparison to prior ages, architecture is now colonized by a very complex and dynamic gaze — or even sets of gazes — that are not just related to a single regime of institutional power.[17] For the first time, the Panoptic imaginary is shot through by an extended eye — a human-machinic prosthesis that actively shifts, sorts and seeks out certain kinds of features, data scrims, and registration marks. It is a gaze that is simultaneously human and inhuman, virtual and real, deliberate and random, institutionally motivated and a naturalized part of habitation. In this way, Panopticism begins to resemble a complex set of concerns associated with the gaze of geomantic divination — or the nexus of natural (biological), ancestral (cultural) and neighborly (community) concerns. This stands in sharp relief to hyper-Panopticism, which is motivated by the unnatural, incestural and colonial concerns of capital rather than qi; of disharmony rather than organic unity; of unmitigated antagonism rather than reciprocity.

And yet, despite these disjunctive dispositif's, a certain degree of similitude exists between 'pan'-opticism and the idea of divination, (or a divine-nation), especially when posited as an identifactory-institutional-structural comport. Afterall, both address how the architecture of vision works to naturalize masculine and feminine roles, worker behavior, familial relations, cultural traditions and every other from of governmentality that undergirds the production and reproduction of (social) life. Both defend the notion that the providence of the nation-state is a matter of great personal and spiritual concern — and both stress the importance of desire in motivating the choices of individuals and communities. But how would we describe the power of the gaze proper to Panopticism and the visual prejudices of Feng Shui in more concrete terms? — in psychoanalytic terms? — or even in mystical/metaphysical terms?

0.9 Lacan and the Architecture of the Gaze: Mirroring Effects, Subjectivation and the Play of (mis)Recognition.

Situating the specificity of these different regimes of subjectivation within the Lacanian idiomatic would mean defining the architecture of the gaze as that particular form of power which produces and reproduces the cultured body through the triangulation of the self, the other, and the big Other — *and yet*, Panoptic power is that singular system of architectural relations constructed around the production of mirroring effects and self-regulating determinations that strive to eliminate or displace the other/Other, (and/or even the otherness within).[18] Panopticism could even be characterized as an infinite power of the self raised to meet its proxy image — in effect, producing an auto-didactic dialectics of self-securing control (self/Self). Beyond just its 'mirroring' effects Panopticism is intimately connected to the Lacanian triad of the imaginary, the symbolic and the real inasmuch as Panoptic reflexivity is a type of doubling that constitutes and is constituted by the material basis of subjectivation vis-à-vis the triangulation of measured distances, the seen and the unseen, (or the structural set up of innumerable effects of misrecognition).

By contrast, Feng Shui can be thought of as a parallogical play of differences that exists somewhere between the tropes of Lacanian psychoanalysis and Panoptic rationalism — or at least as a constitutive gap constituted by the notion of invisible forces, spectral eyes and inter-subjective techniques that fall beyond the purview of psychoanalytic and rationalist imperatives. Feng Shui operates through the terms and conditions provided for by mystico-pragmatico perspectivity — or intuitional practices of reading the gaze of power in place of the little other, the invisible other and the communal other that *in-exists* within an architectural apparatus, i.e., the influence of naturally occurring forms, otherworldly forces and the liminal presence of the neighbor.

0.10 Assemblage Powers and the Concretization of the Mirror Phase: The Social Physics of Observational Perpetuity.

But in counter-distinction to the inscrutable effects associated with the micro-physics of the mirror, the supposed rationality of archio-disciplinary apparatuses and even the group of archio-social practices known as divination, we now find ourselves subjected to the effects of an intensified and scrutinizing techno-architectural assemblage whose sole aim is the seamless functioning and reproduction of the social order — or rather, the reconstruction of social being under the exegesis of hyper-capitalism. As such, the proliferation of new archio-techno-logical machines and advanced networks of surveillance is more than just an extended means of capturing what is visible. Techno-Panopticism consists of refractory procedures that dissect vision in order to cipher it contents and link its positions to intimated provocations. The contemporary diagram of Panoptic control is associated with a condition of visual over-availability that can be thought of as an extension of the mirror phase defined as an allegory about subjectivation — but with the caveat that this schema is finally extended to include the totality of lived existence, (as well as a great deal of imaginary existence).

As a result of this observational perpetuity, we can say that the Pan-*optic* mirror stage is not so much a developmental passage as it is a dispositif of kaleidoscopic categories and networked determinations that are coordinated by so many diffuse forms of systemic, omnipresent and reversible modes of surveillance. Ironically, this dramatic multiplication in ways of seeing and ways of being seen threatens the richness of symbolic existence through the unalloyed transparency of *camera phases* — or the institution of a permanent and open ended 'observational status' grounded in the multiplication of new forms of capture that are more-than-reflective, pragmatic or the mere transcription of a record.

To put it in strictly materialist terms, the camera phase is the concretization of the mirror phase, i.e., the literalization of an allegorical tale about the process of subjectivation failing the symbolic dimension rather than maintaining it, (or at least instituting a new form of symbolic life given over to the facticity of recorded observation). This constricted space of loss and desire has resulted from the concentration, contamination and polycentric interpenetration of social, psychological and concrete apparatuses of subjectivation. In this regard, the collapse of the symbolic dimension is directly related to the elimination of any quantifiable distance between separate dimensions of subjective appropriation — or really, from their sophisticated integration into a tiered apparatus of governance based on the consummate exercise of power.

Feng Shui tries to rehabilitate this lost dimension at the very moment of its collapse because there is finally no difference between mystic contrivances and the mysticism of technology. As Arthur C. Clarke noted long ago 'any sufficiently advanced technology is indistinguishable from magic' — which is why technopticism, (or techno-Panopticism), returns us to a triumphant regime of supersensible control that is coextensive with the machinations of techno-capitalism.[19] Regrettably, it is also a means of infantilizing entire populations of citizenry through the deployment of archio-discipline. Contemporary Panopticism is both the height of judico-legal arrogance and the grandest folly to secure freely productive subjects — an illusory but abiding confidence in sovereign and simulated powers, or simply, Feng Shui's fanciful twin-effect. Everywhere, the intertwining of technology and mysticism, or rather, the mystical dimension produced by complex technologies, makes subjectivation into a system of *installed rule* — and it is increasingly a rule without measure or the necessity of form. This latest mutation in the relationship between technological 'development' and archio-discipline makes the question of resistance today that much harder to grasp, and even tougher to localize or politicize.

0.11 From the Power of 'the Norm' to (im)Perfect Subjects of Discipline: The New Aura of Corrections.

In light of this problematic relationship to technologization, digitization and vitualization, we may have to admit that hyper-Panopticism has finally surpassed the Foucaultian qualification of designating 'normal' and 'abnormal' subjects — as well as making the harmonious subject of mystico-organicism into a figure of ridicule, (a superstitious and irrational proto-proletarian sensibility).[20] In fact, the diagram of architectural power we face today seems oriented toward producing and reproducing perfected and distorted subjects, or really, perfected and imperfect subjects. This is achieved by universalizing a state of mass criminalization where the subject without blemish becomes the exception to the rule.

In such a scenario, the inerrant subject is not the most exalted, the most dignified or even the most revered. Rather, what now defines the providence of the immaculate subject is that he or she is the least identifiable and the least identified within the contemporary context of proliferating techno-pathologies. Absolution in a hyper-Panoptic order means courting the regime of invisibility, or at least having enough money, power and influence to purchase, shape and remake ones public image at will, i.e., to have enough resources to participate in the new economy of auratic corrections.[21] Perfection now is not just the ability to appear blameless in the eyes of others, it also means possessing the ability to vanish from the absolutism of hyper-visibility — even if this can only be achieved reactively. In this optic equation, the indistinct individual and the subject of seamless integration occupy the same relation to public space while being diametrically opposed in socio-economic terms — the wealthy court invisibility while the laymen feels condemned to it — yet both suffer from an indomitable sense of overexposure to invisible forces.

In this context, it is worth noting that Feng Shui was the pre-modern discipline of understanding invisible forces — of being disciplined by invisible forces — and even of disciplining invisible forces. The Feng Shui revival returns to us under these same conditions of suspicion, or really, as a means of resisting conditioned suspicion. Once a description of mystical forces, Feng Shui is now an archio-intuitional means of redressing the auspicious nature of technocratic domination and neo-Panoptic power. Such is the condition of populist resistance to the state sanctioned *panic*-opticism that we find ourselves confronted with today.[22]

FIRST MEDITATION

Neo-Panopticism and the Disciplinary Order of Neo-Liberal Societies

The Panopticon is a utopian vision of society and a kind of power which is, fundamentally, the society we know today, a vision which has been effectively realized. This type of power can perfectly well be called panopticism. We live in a society where panopticism rules.[23]

    Michel Foucault

We should never forget, however, that we are dealing here with the imperial overdetermination of democracy, in which the multitude is captured in flexible and modulating apparatuses of control. This is precisely where the most important qualitative leap must be recognized: from the disciplinary paradigm to the control paradigm of government. Rule is exercised directly over the movements of the productive and cooperating subjectivities; institutions are formed and redefined continually according to the rhythm of these movements; and the topology of power no longer has to do primarily with spatial relations but is inscribed, rather, in the temporal displacements of subjectivities.[24]

    Michael Hardt & Antonio Negri

We are talking about an imaginary of pure, unlimited control, control as it approaches its highest state. That, in its simplest terms, is the *utopia* of telematic orders — the promise land of ultra-infomated, ultra-capitalized, and ultra-cloned societies. Limitless surveillance, perfect simulation. It is also the endgame of those societies, literally, a game of ends — the end of politics, privacy, the social, power, history, war, sexuality, the end of control itself. Here, however, the ends of things are also their beginnings, in the way your genetic code is like a menu of ways to die (pick your disease); in the way virtual reality is the end of one space and the beginning of another, cyberspace; in the way everything about you can be stored on disk and projected over electronic nets, where 'you' disappear, or rather implode into a second surrogate, digital self — an end and a beginning or a beginning with no end or beginning, endlessly replayable, always already played, always already *over* (and over and over again). In these worlds, we have to talk about ecstasies, not just strategies, of control, hypervision and info-power, the ether-police. We have to talk about tele-spies, spaces of absolute vision and the implosion of linear time. We need, in short, a different language to describe the modern cyber-netization of power and discipline.[25]

William Bogard

1.1 Hyper-Mediated Visibility and the Dialectic of Defamation and Rehabilitation: The Passion Play of Panopticism.

The current mutation in the power of visibility, or of the relation of power to visibility, has been explored under many different names and themes, but most recently under the terms of Synopticism (the many watching the one), Banopticism (the many watching the many), and Bio-opticism/electronic Panopticism (Panopticism without technological limit).[26] These three forms of neo-Panopticism offer us concrete event-scenes from which to consider how the contemporary diagram of control operates in the field of architecture, as well as how audio-visual assemblages inform the process of subjectivation, i.e., the process of being and becoming oneself.

Additionally, it is also worth noting that these new models of revisionary Panopticism have pushed the discourse around subjectivation towards a revaluation of the seventeenth century themes of perfection and the damned, the fallen and redeemed, the 'soul-trained' and the malformed spirit. This stands in sharp opposition to the aleatory effects associated with the eighteenth century definition of deviant behavior as adherence to, or departure from, 'the norm'.[27] This new dialectic of defamation and rehabilitation most often accompanies the televised lives of public figures — where news venues and tabloid journalism are both sustained by a quasi-religious dialog that circulates around secularized icons. However, this same transformation in how we speak about social standing and self-knowledge also permeates the discursive texture of day-time talk shows, soap operas, serialized dramas, popular counseling and advice programs, court room and police dramas, etc., etc., — not to mention everyday exchanges about the hyper-visibility of living an all-too-public life. In other words, we have entered an era of theatrical socialization where the spectacular has become a common vernacular — and even a new way of speaking about condemnation and resurrection, where social control is not only a matter of programming and deprogramming individuals, but an invasive practice of politicizing the most intimate forms of information exchange, (audio, visual, textual, etc.).

To paint a picture of this shift in broader strokes means acknowledging how the appearance of a post-Foucaultian Panoptics has worked to naturalize a new series of archio-inter-polative functions in relation to societies of celebrity (Synoptic emulation), (in)security (Ban-optic hysteria) and audio-visual power (Bio-optic invasiveness). But before we can address these dynamic methods of controlling the body socius we must first make an inquiry into the key questions that circumscribe the field of architectural subjection today, namely, what is the focus of these revisionary 'pan'-optics and what changes do they seek to address? How do they move us beyond the considerations of premodern (mystic/sovereign) and modern (Panoptic/disciplinary) power, and perhaps, how do they return us to it in unpredictable and unforeseen ways?

Confronting these contested cartographies of subjectivation throughout the following six meditations will allow us to juxtapose the micro-physics of architectural power with the intuitional metric-management of Feng Shui practices taken as a sign for re-appropriating space and de-expropriating life from the failed functionalism of modern rationality. Or, to put the question on firmer footing, this path of inquiry will allow us to confront the conditions of Panoptic control in the age of completed metaphysics, i.e., of thinking about surveillance societies as a certain form of destinying for the social body, and especially as a type of destinying that must be resisted. However, we must first elucidate the complex (inter-)relation of archiodisciplinary power and its deployment in the social field of exchange, beginning with the three dominant motifs of neo-Panoptic control: Synopticism, Banopticism and Bio-opticism.

1.2 Synopticism, Banopticism and Bio-opticism: Looping, Recursive and Transversal Powers of (post)Panoptic Interpellation.

Undoubtedly, the Synoptic, the Banoptic and Bio-optic are all forms of social physics that offer correctives to the Foucaultian thesis about how power operates in (post)disciplinary societies, or considered much more pragmatically, they are all amendments to Bentham's original design(s). Thus, Synopticism, Banopticism and Bio-opticism are all forms of hyperbolic Panopticism that simultaneously extend and intensify the interpolative powers of subjectivation — albeit with a unique focus on inflection, modulation and minutia, (or the subjectivizing power of commodity customization). Taken together, Synopticism, Banopticism and Bio-opticism form a transversal power of interpellation, or a hyperactive recursive gaze (I see you seeing me seeing you seeing me seeing...) that is divided between multiple regimes of accounting for and cataloging the arena of public bodies, their interactions, their transactions and their circuits of movement. As such, these three forms of revisionary Panopticism can be seen as a sustained effort to describe: (1) how power operates in control societies (post-disciplinary societies) (2) how audio-visual technologies have brought about the end of civil society (privacy rights and the anonymous function of public space) and (3) how the diagram of control associated with Panoptic power functions in relation to archio-audio-visual assemblages (super-structural technopticism).

However, as optical dispositif's, each of these paradigms tends to leave the Acousticon, or one half of the audio-visual assemblage under-theorized — and in many cases, it is simply overlooked altogether.[28] Additionally, bio-surveillance can only be accounted for in any of these schemata in a very tangential manner even though it is directly implicated in the paradigm(s) of electronic/super/hyper-Panopticism.

1.3 Recombant Social Physics and the Duplicitous Gaze of Governmentality: Biopolitics as the Deployment of Optical Techniques.

If we were to strive for a full articulation of how Panoptic power operates in the visible field rather than through visual technologies; and of how the space of Panopticism is sutured to, and constituted by, various architectural motifs; and even of how Panoptic architecture aims to construct a metaphysical dimension of power above and beyond the micro-physics of power, (a move from mere self-regulating power to the neurotic gaze of unceasing self-inspection), then such an inquiry would have to fall under the fourfold designs of the Synopticon, the Banopticon, the Bio-opticon *and* the repressed figure of the Acousticon. In other words, the Panoptic gaze must finally be joined to the ear and the body as a principle of vision, everywhere subjecting public and private space to the principle of law — where bio-politics is constituted by the deployment of bio-optic techniques.

It is these four dispositif's that jointly comprise the paradigm(s) of revisionary, hyperbolic and/or neo-Panopticism — three terms which attempt to describe the same essential transformation. It is also these same themes that put us both before and after Panopticism, i.e., after its completion and before its universalization — or, to be a bit more concise, right in the moment of its radicalization. Panopticism today is synonymous with (1) the intensive subsumption of the visual spectrum by judicio-legal rule, (2) the continuous inspection of the body in the workplace and public life and (3) the naturalization of hyperactive self-inspection and auto-corrective measures derived from the cosmetic world of appearances, the substantive world of inter-subjective relations, the virtual world of data doubles and the familial world of reproductive habits, traditions, etc. Neo-Panopticism, as a designation for the fourfold designs of the Synoptic, the Ban-optic, the Bio-optic and the Acousticon, represents nothing less than a new power of social physics — macro, micro or sub-atomizing — as well as all of their recombant potentialities.

1.4 Immaterial Forms of Subjectivation and New Apparatuses of Capture: Panopticism Without Corporeal Presence, Material Files or Concrete Partitions.

But before we can address this transformation in systems of control; how each of these four thematics are extensions of intensive and extensive systems of Panoptic power; how they each make up but one part of the audio-visual assemblage; how they contribute to defining a power that is more pliant than punitive, more divided than singular, and more diffuse than targeted — it is important to ask why four new forms of

Panopticism have been deployed on the social body at all, or on any body moving through the built environment for that matter — and especially on bodies taken as objects of transit, exchange and verification. Within this horizon of inquiry it is essential to understand what kinds of power gave birth to these new forms of social conditioning, (and anti-social conditioning as the case may be), and whether or not the contemporary diagram of control is really a Panoptic phenomena at all.

Or, to put it somewhat differently, how is the supposed multiplication of Panopticism possible while its three major material impositions, (observational presence, material files and concrete partitions), are on the wane?

1.5 From Social Physics to Meta-Disciplinary Actors: Sub-atomizing Subjectivation and Micro-metric Panopticism.

If the origin of Panoptic power can be located in the desire to operate on subjects unceasingly, and to compel them to internalize the motivational drives that would bind their thoughts and actions to the webbed lattices of the social fabric without anything more than nominal instances of deviation, then today we face a real conundrum. Why wouldn't architectural Panopticism, in its Benthamian incarnation, be enough to accomplish this task? How could there be not just a need for unceasing observation and control but a radical multiplication of the functions and presence of Panoptic power; of its nodal points and nexus effects; of its unconscious operations and its all-to-conscious inscriptions. And how is it that an architecture of totalized and unceasing observation falls short of being able to compel the production of well disciplined subjects, even with the radical institutionalization of hyper-optic control beyond the confines of the penal system? Or, why is the fourfold diagram of subjectivation formed by Synopticism, Banopticism, Bio-opticism and the Acousticon needed at all? What gaps in the micro-physics of power does it aim to secure — and can we call neo-Panopticism a sub-atomizing power that inaugurates an entirely different order of social physics than what adheres to Panopticism proper — perhaps even something more akin to a social metaphysics, or a micro-metric-physics? And how is it that we have moved from architectural and institutional coercion toward interlocking forms of interpolation composed by national, post-national and corporate actors without more than a few passing words of public debate? And how are these meta-disciplinary actors implicated in a million little micro-active displacements, procedures, observations, notations, databases and inquires that occur on a daily basis? And finally, how is all of this related to transformations in the dominant mode of production as well as the working life of labor and day-to-day existence?

1.6 The (paranoiac) Rational of Punishment and Decentered Forms of Power: Subjectivation Between Strong and Weak Models of Correction.

Of course, part of the answer to this particular line of questioning is related to the original failing of the Panopticon itself. It is a well-known fact that Bentham's first proposal was never built — nor his last. But the space of reflection inbetween, where the Panopticon underwent an endless number of revisions in order to court the fancy of private investors and state interests produced the tomb of juridical reference that became *The Rational of Punishment*.[29] And yet, despite these endless attenuations, the exercise of archio-disciplinary power was unable to be realized during the eighteenth century — or at least, it was never actualized using Bentham's architectural designs.

However much it confounded Bentham at the time, every potential backer for the Panoptic penitentiary was capable of grasping how purely rationalist motives lacked the crucial symbolic fortitude of a transcendental signified. The manifold of determinations ascribed to Panoptic surveillance were premised on a reactive rather than an active desire to obey, and that simple fact left its operational efficiency in question. The Panopticon's great problematic was that it was too formal and impersonal a power to be considered viable in the marketplace, and too philosophical a project to be properly understood outside of its concrete applications. Even the purveyors of Enlightenment thought were unwilling to promote a rationalist diagram of power structured around a literal and figurative 'absent center'. This was both its heretical core and the obscene nature of its failure.

The dream of rationalizing observation *always* relied on the full presence of corporeal inspection where nothing could be left to chance; where no act or action could potentially go unseen; where 'rehabilitation' was strictly dependant on a strong power of correction — and where obligatory 'training' wouldn't depend on the supposed efficiency of simulationist techniques, however economically advantageous they were purported to be. In the final analysis, eighteenth century Panopticism amounted to security without watchers, motivated behavior without a strong goal, and a rationalist diagram built for miscreants. What could have appeared more irrational to the determinations of enlightenment thinking than this set of irreconcilable contradictions?

1.7 Four Thesis's on the Rise of Neo-Panoptic Power: Neo-Pragmatism, Secularization, Commercialization and Digitization.

Whether Bentham's philosophy of diagrammatic control proved to be little more than a weak meta-physics, or simply a social physics that couldn't reconcile the chasm between rationalist presuppositions and transcendental qualifiers, a great number of Bentham's observations on power still ring true today. Afterall, it's not so much that his various thesis's only appear plausible in a world of rational actors, but that rationalism remains just one part of understanding subjectivation — and usually, *it is just a bit part*.

But leaving the question of rationally motivated action to the side for a moment, it is also possible to see the return of Benthamian themes as related to the spread of consumerist secularization. With the advent of hyper-capitalism, viral forms of Panopticism become viable at the very same time that techno-cratic consciousness is being elevated to more than just a formal power — everywhere touted as a neo-pragmatic program for the reduction of social ills — and even as a counterbalance to the psychopathologies associated with the process of intensive subsumption.[30]

Or, one could defend the same conclusion by asserting that the opposite is true — that increasing secularization has caused Panoptic control to be raised to a higher power because techno-cratic rule appears that much more empty, unjustified and indefensible in light of its near catastrophic effects on the world around us — and that our concern with hyper-disciplined subjec-tivation has more to do with the eclipse of rationalism than the deployment of reasonable forms of social control.

Against these first two perspectives a third alternative is still possible: that while Bentham's rationalist ideality wasn't powerful enough to compel self-correction and 'soul-training' during the Enlightenment, today's universalized Panopticism has become central to maintaining the motivated irrationalism of consumerist tendencies, where the commercial diagram of power has become dependent on unending observation, inspection and categorization — or what is known in popular terms as 'trending' and/or 'emotional branding'.[31]

And yet, perhaps a fourth answer brings us closest to grasping the real function of hyper-Panoptic control in the twenty-first century — namely, that the rationalist diagram of power has been joined to a transcendent qualifier of sorts, (omnipresence), finally giving Bentham's designs a nearly incontestable, and previously unimagined efficiency. Someone, or really some things, are now always everywhere watching us — posited as the universal implementation of a techno-archio metaphysic. This new 'pan'-optic is constituted by the multiplication of devices of capture such as cameras, scanners, recorders, tracking devices, digital files, imprints, data archives, etc., etc.

As such, neo-Panopticism can be characterized as a system of measures that are *simultaneously* invasive and invisible; active and arbitrary; categorically motivated and open-ended. In this regard, the neo-Panoptic order reconciles many of the contradictions that plagued the Benthamian project by being much more even in its application and far less discontinuous in its distribution — which amounts to saying very much the same thing, i.e., that neo-Panopticism is a power of recuperative univocity.

1.8 Local Determinations, Geometric Derivations and the Instrumental-Architectonics of Social Control: Reading Foucault Reading Bentham on Modern Discipline.

Irrespective of which of the above theses best describes the idea of optical, (or op-technical), control as a new regime of biopower, Bentham is still credited with being the father of the modern prison system and even of being something like the Newton of social physics. His Panoptic program and his description of the function of modern power are still key considerations in the theorization of social control, subjection and subjectivation — if not the centerpiece of such debates. By comparison, Foucault's great contribution is not only to have prepared a place for Bentham in the genealogy of western power that reveals the repressed side of Enlightenment idealism, but also to have made Bentham our contemporary once more by analyzing archio-disciplinary motifs through the lens of micro-physics, (or local determinations). And yet, before addressing the series of innovative readings on Panopticism that continue under the titles of Synopticism, Banopticism, Bio-opticism and the like, it is crucial to reconsider what this supposed system of divisions, distances and demarcations was — how its structures are now spoken of everywhere as if visited — and how Panopticism proposed to institute a new regime of power relations among its subjects, i.e., how it purported to enact an instrumentalized-architectonics of social control.

Or, to get directly at the central question of Panopticism and disciplinary power, it is important to ask just exactly what is the micro-physics of power — both in Bentham's day and our own. This will be the decided theme of our next meditation as well as all that follows.

SECOND MEDITATION

The Micro-Physics of Class Subjectivation

The real value of the punishment constitutes the expense. The apparent value of the punishment influences the conduct of individuals. It is the real punishment that is the expense — the apparent punishment that gives the profit.[32]

Jeremy Bentham

How could we try to analyze power in its positive mechanisms? It seems to me that we can find, in a certain number of texts, the fundamental elements for an analysis of this type. We can find them in Bentham, an English philosopher from the end of the 18th and the beginning of the 19th century, *who was ultimately the great theoretician of bourgeois power,* (my emphasis) and we can obviously find them in Marx, essentially in Volume II of *Capital*. It is there, I think, that we can find several elements on which I can draw for the analysis of power in its positive mechanisms.

In sum, what we can find in volume II of *Capital* is, in the first place, that there exists no single power, but several powers. Powers, which means to say forms of domination, forms of subjection, which function locally, for example in the workshop, in the army, in slave-ownership or in property where there are servile relations. All these are local, regional forms of power, which have their own way of functioning, their own procedure and technique. All these forms of power are heterogeneous. We cannot therefore speak of power, if we want to do an analysis of power, but we must speak of powers and try to localize them in their historical and geographical specificity.[33]

Michel Foucault

29

A science of apparatuses can only be *local*. It can only consist in the regional, circumstantial, and circumstanced mapping of how one or several apparatuses work. Totalization cannot occur without its cartographers' knowing, for rather than in forced systemicity, its unity lies in the question that determines its progress — the question: "How does it work?"

The science of apparatuses competes directly with the imperial monopoly over knowledge powers. This is why its dissemination and communication, the circulation of its discoveries are essentially *illegal*.[34]

Tiqqun

2.1 The Institution of Interrogatory Relations Without Watchers: Panopticism as a System of Auto-Attunement.

Among the numerous descriptions of the Panoptic penitentiary, one of the most succinct comes from the preeminent theorist of surveillance, David Lion. He describes the invention of the diagram of power in Bentham's prison in the following way:

Jeremy Bentham, the British philosopher and social reformer, published his plan for the Panopticon Penitentiary in 1791. Essentially, it was for a building on a semi-circular pattern with an 'inspection lodge' at the center and cells around the perimeter. Prisoners, who in the original plan would be in individual cells, were open to the gaze of the guards, or 'inspectors', but the same was not true of the view the other way. By a carefully contrived system of lighting and the use of wooden blinds, officials would be invisible to the inmates. Control would be maintained by the constant sense that prisoners were watched by unseen eyes. Not knowing whether or not they were watched, but obliged to assume they were, obedience was the prisoner's only rational option. Hence, Bentham's Greek based neologism; the Panoptic, or the 'all-seeing place'.[35]

Here, two points are worthy of note. First, the imaginary of the Panoptic prison is constructed around the idea of housing rational subjects — a sacrosanct and illusionary visage if ever there was one. Today, it goes without saying that any given prison population is calculating, extremely inventive and even incredibly creative, but rarely is it wholly, or even partially, *rational*. This seemingly obvious conclusion was often overlooked in many eighteenth century texts on correctional facilities, and in Bentham's writings in particular.[36]

Second, what is really put into play in Panoptic power is the question of proximity, control and above all else, a *force of suspect invisibility*. The greatest misunderstanding about Foucault's theorization of the micro-physics of power, (or Bentham's writings for that matter), consists of thinking about Panopticism as something of a macro-power made smaller — or, as a micro-physics of power that is still somehow coming from the outside, from the big Other, or big brother, but in qualitatively smaller doses, i.e., as serving size portions of totalitarianism. This reading of the Benthamian-Foucaultian conception of power tends to overlook one key point however — that once a Panoptic relation is put into practice, the observing agent can bow out altogether, or be considered wholly supplemental to the operations of power in a given situation.

As an archio-disciplinary apparatus, Panopticism represents nothing less than a sustained attempt to make power operate without a transcendent qualifier or a corporeal counterpart. Panopticism can only be characterized as a micro-physics of power inasmuch as it operates without any need of physical intercession by trained watchers. In the end, the Panopticon is an architectural apparatus that naturalizes interrogatory relations without necessarily enacting them.[37] It is the vision of a top-down power that is exercised from the bottom up, or even a system of power that has no need of subjective intervention at all — only subjective variation and auto-attunement, (or auto-atonement as Bentham envisioned it).[38]

2.2 From Rational to Emotional Interpellation: The Categorical Subsumption of Subjectivity After Sovereign and Disciplinary Rule.

So if Panopticism inaugurates the micro-physics of self-regulating power in carceral institutions, what is Panoptic power in the broader sense, i.e., in culture at large? How does it circum-scribe the field of inter-subjective relations and subjectivation beyond its local points of influence? What are its attributes, and its effective and affective capacities? How should we define its terms of engagement, its conditions of deployment and its modes of capture? In short, how do we see Panoptic power as initiating a new series of social relations that is markedly different from other forms of power over the body socius?

The answer here is that 'Pan'-optic devices compose an inter-polative force that is exercised through a complex apparatus of observational assemblages — or even that the spread of (neo)Panoptic techniques has given rise to an observational-industrial-complex. Consequently, Panoptic control is conceived of as a relation of the self with the self; as a form of folding subjectivation inward; and as a self-regulating power that is near totalizing for being a discrete model of individuation. Panoptic power compels the subject from the inside — it is neither intended to be coercive nor disciplinary in the sense of physically restraining a body or forcing a body to do anything in particular. As such, Panoptic power is an operative design that is exercised on social relations — deployed and received through a million little particularities, dispensations and imagined rewards — some of which are strongly motivated, and some that are quite imperceptible. Panopticism in its strictly Benthamian incarnation is finally a formal power based on constructing the field of visibility differently — which means that it is imagined as a power that constructs subjects differently. Of course, here the question arises, *differently than what?*

For Bentham, the answer was *different* than the 'vagabond', the 'degenerate', the 'delinquent' and the 'depraved', while Foucault's genealogy points to the idea of (re)defining subjects categorically and historically, i.e., as *other than* subjects of sovereignty. Yet today, we must entertain the thought that hyper-Panopticism might operate in a way that varies, or is even contrary to, how Foucault describes its eighteenth century counterpart:

Hence, the major effect of the Panopticon: to induce in the inmate a state of conscious and permanent visibility that assures the automatic functioning of power. So to arrange things that the surveillance is permanent in its effects, even if it is discontinuous in its action; that the perfection of power should tend to render its actual exercise unnecessary; that this architectural apparatus should be a machine for creating and sustaining a power relation independent of the person who exercises it; in short, that the inmates should be caught up in a power situation of which they themselves are the bearers. To achieve this, it is at once too much and too little that the prisoner should be constantly observed by an inspector: too little, for what matters is that he knows himself to be the one observed, too much, because he has no need in fact of being so. In view of this, Bentham laid down the principle that power should be visible and unverifiable. Visible: the inmate must never know whether he is being looked at at any moment; but he must be sure that he may always be so. In order to make the presence or absence of the inspector unverifiable, so that the prisoners, in their cells, cannot even see a shadow, Bentham imagined not only venetian blinds on the windows of the central observation hall, but, on the inside, partitions that intersected the halls at right angles and, in order to pass from one quarter to the other, not doors but zig zag openings; for the slightest noise, a gleam of light, a brightness in the half-opened door would betray the presence of the guardian. The Panopticon is a machine for dissociating the see/being seen dyad: in the periphery ring, one is totally seen, without ever seeing; in the central tower, one sees everything without ever being seen.

It is an important mechanism, for it atomizes and disindividualizes power. Power has its principle not so much in a person as in a certain concentrated distribution of bodies, surfaces, lights, gazes; in an arrangement whose internal mechanisms produce the relation in which individuals are caught up. *The ceremonies, the rituals, the marks by which the sovereign's surplus power was manifested are useless* (my emphasis). There is a machinery that assures dissymmetry, disequilibrium, difference. Consequently, it does not matter who exercises power. Any individual, taken almost at random, can operate the machine: in the absence of the director, his family, his friends, his visitors, even his servants (Bentham, 45). Similarly, it does not matter what motives drive him: the curiosity of the indiscreet, the malice of a child, the thirst for knowledge of a philosopher who wants to visit this museum of human nature, or the perversity of those who take pleasure in spying and punishing. The more numerous those anonymous and temporary observers are, the greater the risk for the inmate of being surprised and greater his anxious awareness of being observed. The Panopticon is a marvelous machine which, whatever use one may wish to put it to, produces homogenous effects of power.[39]

It is here that we find a truly modern innovation within the regime of Panopticism, being an apparatus that addresses 'difference' in order to 'produce homogenous effects of power'.

And yet, if we were to compare hyper/neo-Panopticism with its eighteenth century predecessor, it would mean describing the very production of difference as a homogenizing effect — absurdist individualism, globanality, the atomizing of particularities as a function of (dis)similitude — or worse yet, of accessing the loss of any totalizing horizon which could understand difference in qualitative terms. The enigmatic nature of neo-Panopticism is closely tied to the production of heterogeneous affects that erode the difference between self-valorization and auto-valorization, and thus, *the difference attributed to difference itself.* In contrast to Panopticism proper, Neo-Panopticism is a diagram of extreme torque applied to sonorous being, only it is weighted toward emotional rather than rational interpellation, or toward desire rather than discipline. That is why neo-Panopticism is a subjectivizing process based on motivated consumerism rather than consumptive needs — it approbates subjects differently by tailoring itself to projected designs. The proper name for neo-Panopticism might finally be eclectic Panopticism: a power of control exercised in relation to the desire for unique individualism in an era of grand uniformity — a subjectivizing force of absolutist neo-narcissism aimed at the categorical subsumption of all singularity.

2.3 Eight Challenges to Panopticism: The Diagram of Discipline Reconsidered.

But once again, we are confronted with the question, why wasn't Panoptic control enough — and why didn't it function even in the setting for which it was intended — and is neo-Panopticism ultimately slated for the same fate? Here we could defer to some of the problems mentioned already, i.e., that prisoners are in no way compelled to behave as rational actors; that the Enlightenment could not take its own presuppositions seriously; that Panopticism lacked a strong power of interpellation, etc.. Or, we could cite some of its many technical problems: that the

Panopticon was simply too complex and expensive a structure to build and maintain; that problems such as the two way monitoring of audio conversations and the impracticality of glass walled cells plagued the structure throughout, or even that its multiform orientations actually confounded the perception of rational and clear organization — not to mention strictly functional concerns outside of hierarchical observation, like walking the prisoners to and fro down diagonal halls and sharp turns.

While these are perhaps the most transparent and undeniable reasons for the failure of eighteenth century Panopticism, understanding the rise of networked Panopticism today requires an extended examination of Bentham's shortcomings. Fortunately, the surveillance critic Kevin D. Haggerty has provided us with eight key theses about the contradictions and paradoxes of (neo)Panoptic power. They are, in no particular order of importance, the following: (1) Panoptic modes of control in no way account for the enjoyment of being watched — for the pleasure prisoners take in flashing guards and making obscene gestures of all sorts — or even just the perverse hope of lying in wait to be observed. (2) Panoptic power really has no way of theorizing the scrutiny of the powerful which tries to capture "documentary traces" and "aggregate trends" in social patterning that reinforce simple forms of emulation and hero worship, i.e., the desire to be like the watchers.[40] (3) Pre-modern Panopticism also cannot provide a model for understanding the sheer volume of surveillance, both human and non-human, that occurs today vis-à-vis data tracking services, disease control agencies and the imaging of inorganic bodies. This would require something like a theory of non-sentient Panopticism or a Panoptic infomatics. (4) As a paradigm for understanding contemporary power relations, Panopticism finds itself challenged by the proliferation of different types of surveillance and the ubiquitous absence of motivated watchers in these new diagrams of control. (5) This last point leads us to a more pressing question for Panoptic practices, namely, what are the roles of the remaining watchers outside of just watching — both in Bentham's day and our own? And what is their relation to perceptivity, judico-legal regulations, security assemblages and so on and so forth? What is to be done in light of a violation of protocol — and what system of retaliation, reformation and remuneration would make Panopticism appear more or less effective? (6) It also seems as if Bentham overlooked the difference between extensive and intensive training, or what Freud would later call conscious motivation and unconscious sublimation. As such, it is hard to understand how a regime of training works without a stated purpose or goal — or even if this can plausibly be called 'training' at all, much less 'soul-training'. (7) We shouldn't entirely disavowal the positive effects of Panopticism either, but there is a need to account for how, when, where and why such powers might be deployed as well as what conditions would make their use acceptable within the paradigm of modern democracy. (8) Last but not least, isn't it possible that Foucault's late turn toward governmentality was his way of overcoming these contradictions and omissions? Could it be that in Foucault's later work the paradigm of Panopticism appears as something of a relic in trying to describe the contemporary diagram of power — or at the very least, that it has already begun to look like an outmoded cartography of sorts?

2.4 Contradiction and Complexity in the Social Field of Exchange: The Paradoxes of Panopticism Today.

Here we finally come up against the central paradox of power in the expanded field of social exchange(s): why is it, that if Panopticism is divided by innumerable contradictions, both in Bentham's day and our own, that it is still a serviceable paradigm for conjecture about how power motivates the process of subjectivation? What qualifies its continued usage more than two centuries after Bentham's writings on the subject? And has

Panopticism been replaced by a diagram of control that issues from something other than the premises of revisionary/hyperbolic/neo-Panopticism? Is Panoptic power just a McGuffin in the classic sense of being a contentless plot motivator as Baudrillard suggested in *Forget Foucault?*[41] Afterall, it does seem as if Bentham's designs for social physics work on everything but penitentiary control. As such, the key question concerning how we understand (bio)power and its relation to the body socius continues to depend on whether or not Panopticism can still be considered a useful concept outside of its eighteenth century context — and what, *if anything*, constitutes its critical purchase in the present?

2.5 Reorganizing Productivity and Social Being: Panopticism as a Form of Architectural Abstraction and Subjective Appropriation.

Before directly addressing the innovations, modifications and mutations that have taken place with regard to Panoptic power, (the Synoptic, the Banoptic, the Bio-optic and the Acousticon), it is important to highlight one last reason why Bentham remained the repressed voice of rationalist power well into the twentieth century — and ultimately, why his project was capable of being renewed under so many different names and techniques today. For all its philosophic presuppositions the Panopticon was still seen as being too much of a *thing* in the eighteenth century, (and a really impractical brick and mortar thing at that), rather than a complex series of interlocking social relations that (re)organize productivity, and by proxy, subjectivity. Without this secondary qualifier, its symbolic, economic and structural efficiency would always appear to be compromised from within — an experiment not worth undertaking.

Much like capitalism, (which depends on turning every object of production into a thing that conceals the social relations behind its appearance as a commodity-form), Panopticism also sets up and reinforces a series of social relations by type and kind that actively conceal its function as an architectural diagram. Panopticism is not so much a socializing architecture as it is *an architecture that produces social-forms*. In other words, Panopticism qualifies and maintains exploitative and/or demonstrative relations of social power through a process of architectural abstraction. This is how Panopticism creates surplus value — by adapting to the limitless potential of subjective appropriations.[42] This is the hidden dimension of Panopticism that was obscured by Bentham's focus on 'real' and 'apparent' value as well as being the defining socio-economic concern that Foucault only alluded to in the most oblique manner.[43] But there is also a rather practical reason why this oversight occurred — a reason that only comes into view with the advent of the hyper-capitalist mode of production.

2.6 Neo-Panopticism and the New Regime of Labor: Hyperbolic Capitalism and Affective Forms of Subjectivation.

While the orchestration of the Panoptic gaze presented all the great hopes of rationalist exchange as open to endless forms of subordination, subjection and exploitation, its use-value in the eighteenth century remained indeterminate because work was largely discontinuous. As such, its efficiency, adaptability and hard cash value could not be accounted for beyond basic forms of regimentation and coercion. This is because Panoptic control engenders any number of reaction formations; Panopticism overcodes every type of social exchange even when nothing is exchanged; Panopticism is even a relation of non-exchanges where architectural motifs become a stand-in for the big Other, and transference is displaced from individuals onto the whole of society and its organizational powers. In the eighteenth century Panopticism was not a regime of clear and quantifiable exchanges but a *mixed regulator* at best. Panoptic techniques hadn't come to fruition in Bentham's day because formal subsumption (pre-industrial and industrial capital) is a *hard regulator* — a qualifier for determinations of energy and output, mass and matter, force and time — rather than affective processes of subjectivation.

Consequently, Panopticism's continuing influence relies on the fact that it represents a system of relations that are increasingly based on the production of a subject rather than a thing, or worse yet, of a thing taken for a subject — or even, the creation of all-too-thingly-subjects. Panoptic control is finally not so much the bastard child of the Enlightenment but the prodigal son of mercantile capitalism welcomed home by its pedophilic stepfather, hyperbolic capitalism, (the illicit touching of indo-colonization). Panoptic schematization really addresses the subject of class rather than the subject of classification — or it posits class-i-fication as a condition of class warfare by naturalizing disciplinary designs under the rubric of 'personal responsibility' and 'moral improvement', i.e., the production of the self as self-reproduction, auto-appropriation and dead-labor.

Is this the defining motif behind Panoptic power which Bentham so readily overlooked as well as the untenable inheritance of Enlightenment thought that Foucault was quick to downplay — or at the very least, to contentious leave aside?[44] And if so, how are we to think about this gap in the constitution of Panoptic power and its ability to make social divisions invisible? How is it that the *'pan'*-optic proposes to operate on all subjects with the same quality of force while individuating its techniques of expropriation? And how are we to account for the move from the disciplined individuation of Panoptic control to the hyper-dividuation of neo-Panopticism, other than through the increasing reification of consciousness?

2.7 Panopticism and Transformations in Political Economy: From Deterministic to Integral Models of Value.

Overlooking the simplistic use of prisons for the correction and training of the lower classes (the mass of lumpenproletariat), and the Panoptic re-organization of the industrial workplace (for the proletariat proper), means moving beyond a reductive conception of class power as en-*forced* rule and simple socio-economic stratification. These forms of disciplinary control are not necessarily applicable to the post-industrial workplace and the powers of subjectivation that attend its subjects. Instead, neo-Panoptic power has to be triangulated in relation not only to the metaphysics of presence, i.e., to how the transcendental signified of big brother as the big Other is enacted at a material level — but also in regard to how a near super-sensible power of subjec-tivation operates in the field of indentifactory appropriations constituted by 'social standing'.

Of course, Panopticism effects the celebrity class and other public figures on a much more self-conscious level than the layman. It holds an entirely different set of concerns for the criminal class, the revolutionary, the dissident and the rural fundamentalist. It is a kind of informed watching for the corporate aristocracy, the leisure class and the members of gated communities who enjoy and even rely on the active deployment of Panoptic assemblages to qualify divisions of privilege and protectionism. And while there exist many other noteworthy Panoptic relations that highlight class divisions, what Bentham could not understand, and what has sustained the discourse of Panopticism for over two centuries, is that Panoptic power produces an endless number of subjective and subjectivizing processes — but increasingly these have more to do with capital and control than incarceration and correction — especially as capitalism has extended and transformed its appropriative mechanisms.[45] Yet, describing this transformation as a historical sequence, or even as a series of overlapping sequences, is no simple endeavor.

One of the most timely contributions to such a project comes from the media theorist Toshimaru Ogura who has provided a succinct description of the social, economic and technological transformations that make a materialist reading of (neo)Panopticism possible. For Ogura, this means acknowledging five distinctive shifts not only in the mode of production, but also in the organizational apparatuses that accompany different modes of production. His analysis of the subsumption of labor by capital is quoted here at length for its relevance to the advent of neo-Panopticism today:

> (First Layer)
> Modern surveillance-oriented society has five historical layers. The base layer was formed around the eighteenth century in Western countries, especially England as a country of the first industrial revolution. Its social structure, in terms of management of the population, was an urban-industrial labour power which was a new phenomena of population entirely different from rural populations. The working class was regarded as a 'dangerous' class. The creation of workplace surveillance technology was designed to dissolve skilled labour into unskilled labour and to replace workers with machines. From the Industrial Revolution in the nineteenth century to the ICT-oriented (Information Communication Technology) society of the late twentieth century, workplace control has been a common interest of capitalism. Surveillance meant that capitalists could keep watch over the behavior of manual workers in factories. Both the deskilling and the segmentation of labour and the replacement of workers with machines were the result of the capitalist motive *to control the human body from the outside* (my emphasis)...[46]

(Second Layer)

The second historical layer appeared in the late nineteenth century, when the management of the population was extended beyond the factory nationwide. Beyond this, one can argue that democracy and colonialism are two sides of the same coin. The universal suffrage movement and labour movement in imperial countries, and more sophisticated management of the population in colonies, occurred simultaneously. In western European countries that were in the age of classical imperialism, *surveillance technology was extended to everyday life* (my emphasis). Social policy gradually emerged for the integration of unemployment and low-income classes into the nation state. A 'carrot and stick' policy was adopted, where the majority of the working class was integrated into the capitalist order by the legalization of trade unions and the development of social policy for the unemployed. On the other hand, socialists, anarchists and other subversive parts of the working class were excluded. Prejudice based on race and gender was strengthened by the science of crime. Criminology, based on the use of physical features, was invented, which downplayed the impact of social circumstances in crimes. In colonial regions, the native population was managed in different ways than in imperial countries. Fingerprint and other classical biometric identifiers were introduced to manage the population...[47]

(Third Layer)

The Third layer appeared in the Cold War era. Surveillance as a tool to manage the population spread from the control of appearance to *the control of the human mind* (my emphasis). While women, ethnic minorities and other social groups were requiring their own rights, the dominant strategy used to control identity politics was to integrate these groups into a high consumer society called 'affluent society', based on the

Keynesian policy of income redistribution. Surveillance became an extension into constructing the consumer's life, although identifying each individual as an inherent subject was difficult. Unknown consumers were regarded as an element of an unknown mass to be monitored. Mass media and advertising became two of the major tools of mind manipulation, making people in developed countries look as though they enjoy freedom and democracy...[48]

(Fourth Layer)

The fourth socio-historical layer resulted from the crisis of control and surveillance-based mass consumption and mass democracy. The decentralization of mass workers and mass consumers was introduced by computerization as hi-mix, low-volume production systems, based on the availability of computer-processing-based marketing. Mass consumption, which was the social background of what Herbert Marcuse called the 'one-dimensional man', and other critiques of uniform consumer society were out of date (Marcuse 1964). Mass anonymous consumers were dissolved into various consumer groups and even individuals. Diversity based on identity politics was taken over by the market economy, commodification of diversity, and the rediscovery of individuals with proper names based on marketing (identifactoy socialization — my addition)...[49]

(Fifth Layer)

The fifth layer is based on ICT, emerging at the end of the Cold War and continuing until the present. Dissemination of the Internet and cell phones brings the reconstruction of previous layers of surveillance (or what I term the post-historical condition — my addition). In the 1990s, the Internet was commercialized and institutionalized as a social infrastructure. Its forerunner was 'The Information

Superhighway', a term coined by the administration of U.S. president Bill Clinton. The dissemination of ICT for identification and certification spread from welfare to policing and national security activities. So-called electronic government... is the necessary result of this layer. E-government aims to redefine human identity by introducing networked databases, certification agent systems, identity cards, radio-frequency identification (RFID) and biological identification technology such as bio-metrics. Another important aim of e-government is to import administration methods of the commercial sector so that the administrative structure of government is regarded as the same as that of a commercial company (intensive subsumption — my addition). This significantly strengthens the surveillance power of government while democracy based on anonymity becomes weak.[50]

As Ogura is quick to point out, his genealogy does not describe the discrete progression of different powers of surveillance but the *thoroughgoing integration of past layers*. Ogura also has to be credited with noting how neo-Panoptic regimes find traditional rationalism displaced by a machinic view of the unconscious that reveals "a deep skepticism toward humans... modern/postmodern society inherently has a kind of machine fetishism at the core of its worldview. It assumes, therefore, that being human lies at the root of uncertainty, that machines are without error, and that following instructions faithfully is an ideal model of humans." [51] In this way, the conflict between Enlightenment thought and postmodern cynicism is reconciled through the desire for excessive control, the escalation of labor-time and the development of integral rather than deterministic models of value. Within this system of highly motivated antagonism(s), irrational suspicion comes to mirror the irrationality of (hyperbolic) capitalism, where the smooth space of Panoptic control can be said to overcode the striated space of class conflict by concealing a perverse reciprocity between epistemes that were once considered to be diametrically opposed. In this way neo-Panopticism reveals itself to be something of a dialectical force, or a hyperbolic form of synthetic appropriations and recombant powers — or simply a historical hybrid effect based on the drive for capitalist accumulation beyond equitable proportion, i.e., as a force complementary to hyper-expropriation, hyper-accumulation and hyper-exploitation.

2.8 Subjectivation as a Distributed Force of Social Stratification: Panopticism and Determination in the First Instance.

And yet, if we were to name the domain of power proper to Panopticism and class — or the place where Panoptic control is perceived to be an (re)active force of subjection and subjectivation — then one would have to say that Panopticism has its greatest effect on those with the most to lose rather than the least! In this regard, the operations of neo-Panopticism are closer to representing the radical inversion of Bentham's original presuppositions. Or, to avoid such a simplistic reduction, one could characterize Panopticism as a force that territorializes its subjects in relation to socio-economic divisions while being especially effective on those who reside above the poverty line.

This is perhaps, the singular reason that Panopticism cannot be so easily dismissed from our understanding of contemporary power, and especially from the fourfold diagram of networked Panopticism that continues to expand its influence over local, national and international actors. Panopticism is a form of control in relation to class politics; it is a dynamic dossier of data-veillance that awaits criminals to be; it is a power of pre-criminalization posited as a reforming tool for every kind of 'abnormal' and/or 'imperfect' behavior; it is even, a profoundly retroversive effect that determines subjectivation in the first instance rather than the last. The effectivity of Panopticism tends to function in direct relation to how unseen a subject feels — but it is only fully manifest, (without interruption), as a power of double invisibility, i.e., as a disavowed relation. This is its power of abstraction over class and economic relations; over personal and public actors; over the politics of access and identification; and over the implicit and explicit injunctions of (re)production.

Once Panopticism becomes anything else, namely a self-conscious or even pseudo-self-conscious relation, it is distributed through an entirely different means — namely, the power of the prohibition which enacts the draw of the taboo. This other type of Panopticism, if it can still be called that, subjectivizes by creating the desire for its own subversion. But is Panopticism any less effective for all this? Has the move from concrete partitions to virtual divisions disrupted its operative effects? Is Panopticism still an adequate force of interpolation and subjectivation for having to rely so strongly on imaginary and/or simulated relations?

2.9 Panopticism and Socio-Psychological Expropriation: Documentation Without Directive as the Central Motif of the Neo-Colonial Enterprise.

In Bentham's day the answer would have been yes — Panopticism constantly undermines its own ends by limiting and defining its propositions too clearly. In our day the answer is no — the Panoptic regime builds on the necessity for its own expansion through those who active defy its presence, (whether by fetish, perversion, or even serendipity), and it acts that much more concretely on those who embrace its all-securing gaze. This tends to occur for two distinct reasons: (1) Panopticism is first and foremost a diagram of subjective and subjectivizing accommodations, and (2) Panopticism today is wholly post-penitentiary. It knows no limits, and with the rise of technocracy, it finally knows no physical, architectural or judico-legal constraints.

Under Bentham's designs Panoptic power was never anything more than a series of concrete relations deployed on a limited population where the issue of control could never be naturalized, and as a consequence, it was often neutralized. Today it is finally totalized — everywhere reaching its greatest point of intensification. Unlike its eighteenth century incarnation, neo-Panopticism has the added dimension of technological extension where 'examination' functions through the complex integration and manipulation of devices of capture. No one needs to have the feeling of being examined anymore because they are simply taken-in, conspicuously absorbed and documented without directive. Panopticism, in becoming post-architectural, is completed through the pervasiveness of uninterrupted watching, naturalized surveillance and the incalculable perspectivism of an immaterial all-seeing electronic gaze.

In this regard, neo-Panopticism is not a series of traits but a distinctive superadded effect. The project of Panopticism is just now nearing its completion because self-regulating techniques of social stratification have been naturalized on both sides of the penitentiary walls, subtly dividuating subjects by class, taste, social standing, hobbies, infractions, etc. The greater problem however, is not just that every form of architecture can be colonized and reterritorialized for Panoptic ends through the implementation of audio-visual devices. The real issue at hand is that this happens *regardless* of whether or not the diagram of control is posited as a structural necessity, a safety measure or an aesthetic effect. Increasingly, every architecture bares the mark of Panoptic presuppositions — most of which have been designated as principles of 'effective' design, i.e., the knowledge and placement of easily identified subjects, clear hierarchies of command, and obvious divisions of social and professional standing. But more importantly, neo-Panopticism has been naturalized as a way to create the feeling of (in)security irrespective of whether or not it actually achieves this goal. Such is the horizon of the neo-colonial/indo-colonial enterprise today — an activity of subjective trespass which lacks both an identifiable outside or any form of internal delimitation. In this regard, what we face a today is a kind of (neo)Panopticism unbound, or a regime of socio-political control which is becoming immeasurable.

THIRD MEDITATION

The Crisis of Capitalist Control at the End of History

Time is out of joint. The world is going badly. It is worn but its wear no longer counts. Old age or youth — one no longer counts in that way. The world has more than one age. We lack the measure of the measure. We no longer realize the wear, we no longer take account of it as a single age in the progress of history... The age is off its hinges. Everything, beginning with time, seems out of kilter, unjust, dis-adjusted. The world is going very badly, it wears as it grows... the picture is bleak...[52]

    Jacques Derrida

Marx did not elaborate a theory of time adequate to his idea of history... the fundamental contradiction of modern man is precisely that he does not yet have an experience of time adequate to his idea of history, and is therefore painfully split between being-in-time as an elusive flow of instants and his being-in-history, understood as the original dimension of man. The twofold nature of every modern concept of history, as *res gestae* and as *historia rerum gestarum,* as diachronic reality and as synchronic structure which can never coincide in time, express this inability of man, who is lost in time, to take possession of his own historical nature.[53]

    Giorgio Agamben

By its very nature, capital can be nothing but control, since it is constituted through an alienated objectification of the function of control, as a reified body apart from and opposed to the social body itself... Today, however, we witness the emergence of a fundamental contradiction, with the gravest possible implications for the future of capitalism: for the first time in human history the unhampered dominance and expansion of the inherently irrational capitalist structures and mechanisms of social control are being seriously interfered with by pressures arising from the elementary imperatives of mere survival... For the first time in history capitalism is confronted with its own problems, which cannot be postponed much longer.[54]

István Mészáros

3.1 Neo-Panopticism and the Rise of Control Societies: Axial Relations of Power and Audio-Visual Techniques.

In light of the changes in power associated with hyper-capitalism, we still need to come up with a plausible answer as to why four new forms of revisionary Panopticism are needed at all, what they aim to achieve at the level of praxis and what gaps and fissures in architectural Panopticism they attempt to cover over. Second, it is important to address what kind of power is constituted by the fourfold designs of neo-Panopticism: totalitarian, coercive, diffuse, fluctuating, indistinct, etc.? And finally, we will need to return to the premise of this inquiry in searching for new forms of resistance to Panopticism that are already operative and gaining ground — such as populace practices of reorganizing private and public space like Feng Shui.

But these concerns cannot be addressed in isolation, rather, it is necessary to try to articulate their interrelatedness along a very specific set of axial relations, namely, (1) what is the difference between disciplinary societies and control societies, (2) how is the latter composed of extensive and intensive diagrams of control, and (3) what is an audio-visual technology?

3.2 From Extensive Regimes of Control to Intensive Apparatuses of Investment: Affective Labor, Intensive Subsumption and Indo-Colonization.

The first answer to this particular line of questioning is not that hard to convey because it mirrors the logic of capitalist 'development'. Where industrial (disciplinary) capitalism was an extensive regime, everywhere ordering the body, its motions, its periods of exertion and rest, etc., postmodern or post-industrial capitalism is an apparatus of intensive investment and control — the expropriation of knowledges, technologies, emotional states and even bio-matter. While disciplinary societies were focused on inventing new modes of manufacture, societies of control are largely concerned with manipulating different modes of information. The first of these two forms of social organization is largely a regime of colonialism, the second, of internalized colonization — or indo-colonization.[55] Yet, the major difference that divides disciplinary societies from control societies is that the first 'trains' and 'corrects' bodies while the second expands the means by which a body selects the same set of motivations through dis-identification with everything that doesn't contribute to the reproduction of the capitalist order. Or, to put it somewhat more succinctly, disciplinary societies are concerned with the expropriation of surplus value created by physical labor while societies of control are focused on strategies of rapid accumulation based on the subsumption of ideas, affections, language and all other forms of immaterial labor.[56]

3.3 The Four Regimes of Social Control: Mystical, Sovereign, Disciplinary and Subjectivizing.

While these principal determinations highlight the differences between two dissonant regimes of capital, a longer view of the presuppositions of power and its relationship to production is still necessary in order to explain the distinctive characteristics of disciplinary mechanisms. In contrast to mystical interpolation, which draws its allegiance from superstition and the power of suggestion — or sovereignty, which produces public spectacles around the forced exercise of power over and against the body — Foucault describes disciplinary regimes as constituted by "the use of simple instruments; hierarchical observation, normalizing judgment and their combination in a procedure that is specific to it, the examination."[57] In Foucault's genealogy of western power it is disciplinary apparatuses, and Panoptic mechanisms in particular, that represent a qualitative mutation in the exercise of social control. Born of a failing belief in religious authority and metaphysical demagoguery, Panopticism's chief function was "to 'train', rather than select and to levy; or, no doubt, to train in order to levy and select all the more."[58]

And yet, in the wake of Foucault's work, the philosopher Gilles Deleuze defended the position that a much more dramatic revolution in power was already well underway — and that Panoptic discipline had reached its apotheosis during the industrial era. This was no small claim, and one which threatened to displace the terms of modern power relations in their entirety. But how was this transformation posited — what new apparatuses and figures of subjection accompanied its appearance — and how was it qualitatively different than the forms of social control it claimed to surpass?

3.4 The 'Monetary Mole' and the 'Control Man': Subjectivation Between Industrial and Post-Industrial Capitalism.

For Deleuze technological production gave rise to the 'control man' — the undulating, serpentine and continuous producer of speculative profits and precarious social relations.[59] This post-disciplinary figure stood in sharp opposition to the 'monetary mole' of discontinuous production and protracted upward mobility.[60] As such, the erratic dividual of control societies presupposes a greater need for systems of domination than the disciplinary subject proper — being *both* a more unstable and modulated subject — repressed by variation rather than force; by difference rather than homogeneity; by over-availability rather than restriction. The 'monetary mole' always dug in, committed to local businesses and national brand names; to climbing the corporate ladder; to familial relations and familiar routines, whereas the 'control man' was part of an entirely different model of social normativity — one who's core traits were networking, undercutting and streamlining production; seeking out the perfected means of profiteering; and valorizing unrestricted opportunism and rapid accumulation. Unlike the 'monetary mole', the 'control man' saw no contradiction in lobbying for the consolidated influence of economic power(s) over every aspect of contemporary life: governance, education, militarism, health and even inter-subjective relations. With the rise of post-industrial/transnational capital, the prospects of radical deregulation and the defense of the 'divine hand of the market' became the call of the day – the 'control man's' *cri d'ames*.

Where the 'monetary mole' was circumscribed by a slow incremental burrowing process called industrialization, 'progress', or even *modernity*, the 'control man' was used to short-term commitments, perpetual travel, corporate restructuring, office politics, social angling and furtive alliances — a becoming-corporate-animal or reified-raider mentality focused only on the hope of quick returns and dramatic gains. The 'control man' was a disciple of post-industrial techniques — technologization, financialization, spectacularization and speculation. Often called the 'creative' or the 'executive' class, this new group of producers lacked the same set of commitments as the 'monetary mole' — but with good reason.[61] Maintaining 'control', in this instance, often meant surviving the radical destructuration of *all environs*, (nation-state, public institutions, the home, etc.), and especially the places and functions associated with hard production and secure employment. This quasi-schizoid subject witnessed the rise of liquid capitalism or what Zygmunt Bauman has defined as *liquid modernity* — a period "where all patterns of dependency and interaction... are now malleable to an extent unexperienced by, and unimaginable for, past generations."[62] Unlike the subject of modern industrialization, the 'control man' laid no claim on 'development', but only on developing the potential of over-capacity, planned obsolescence and unrestricted profiteering. In short, the 'control man' accepts economic Darwinism in light of the failing prospects of economic determinism.

But is this the sole reason for increased repression today — that it is harder than ever to convince people that things are going well and that they should work even harder than before to secure the gains of a system that is imploding, or at least, entering a stage of entropic decay? Is the production of a subject distorted by generalized insecurity, progressive pharmaceutical-ization and the universalization of worker time the reason that hyperbolic Panopticism has become defensible to 'society' at large? Or, is it even a bit more complicated than the contradiction between working harder and working longer for nascent compensation and compromised social mobility — not to mention the unfortuitous liquidation of the natural world? Is there still a greater enigma to unfold than the collapse of all long-term planning — or even the radical devaluation of self-preser-vation?

3.5 Networked Apparatuses of Capture and Polymorphous Forms of Metabolic Attenuation: The Crisis of Accelerated (re)Production, Dead(ening) Labor and Social Atomization.

What is rarely grasped in the move from tribal and nomadic trade (mystical power) to preindustrial/agrarian production (sovereign power) to industrial/monopoly capitalism (disci-plinary societies) to post-industrial and transnational exchange policies (control societies), is that the fourth revolution in capitalist power — the movement underway today — is itself a *non-movement* (anti-linear, anti-teleological, anti-historical). Rather, the opening moment of hyperbolic/affective capitalism is defined by a recursive gesture that folds the previous four diagrams of production and control into one another. In this regard, the generalized crisis of power and its exertion on the social field of (re)production has everywhere caused a dramatic redoubling of sorts — a dynamic synthesis of all past forms rather than their overcoming. This *supernova effect* fuses mystical, sovereign, disciplinary and technological apparatuses in a four pronged effort to overdetermine (1) the state of cultural tribalism known as pluralism; (2) the spread of neo-feudal economics associated with the rise of ground and technological rents; (3) the consolidation of neo-sovereign power in relation to the 'state of exception' in western democracies and; (4) the further development of systemic forms of techno-Panopticism, i.e., intensive techniques of social modulation.

In other words, an apportioned power is deployed in relation to the relative degree of variance in the organization of a social body — instituted and qualified as it is by affective capitalism — — or really, power is deployed in order to secure the (re)production of (in-)dividuated anti-social bodies through the wild proliferation of polymorphous apparatuses of metabolic and psychological attenuation.

Another way of saying the same thing is that the Synoptic, the Banoptic, the Bio-optic and the Acousticon are all a means of addressing the mixed constitution of post-historical existence and its uneven modes of production, i.e., of accelerating the production and reproduction of every type of exploitive power in relation to the maximal moment of socio-economic disparity that characterizes contemporary life. Uneven development is itself, *the key social factor that begets the end of history* — the loss of concord between nations, peoples and equitable terms of labor, production and exchange. Regrettably, the abandonment of teleological goals doesn't result in the spread of unlimited freedom and a new openness to all that is. Quite the opposite, it returns us to the radical mobilization of all regimes of control at all times and all places as a precautionary measure set against every potential form of resistance to the expropriation of life, energy and monetary gain.

But what else, beyond just the heterogeneity of exploitative powers, is motivating the need for absolutist control? What other forces of interpellation need to be accounted for in the diagram of net-*worked* social stratification?

3.6 Capitalist Deterritorialization After Deleuze: From the Crisis of Enclosures to the Crisis of Foreclosures.

While there are many different phenomena that inform the growing exercise of bio-power today — from post-industrial production and the universalization of capitalist time; to the death of the self-determined and self-determining subject; or the end of history and teleology; and even the rise of terrorism and nuclear/biological warfare — it is the work of Gilles Deleuze which provides an acute diagnosis of how control societies address a very specific socio-economic predicament. In no uncertain terms, this is the crisis of "environments of enclosure — prison, hospital, factory, school, family" that occurred after World War II.[63] But what undergirds this socio-economic problematic and what are its essential features, its points of unmitigated antagonism and its expropriative sequences? How are we to think the crisis of enclosures in their entirety — or to put it in Jameson's terms, how can such a transformation be 'cognitively mapped'?[64]

While any answer to the totality of problems associated with hyperbolic capital is bound to be inconclusive, a general cartography of these issues must still be attempted in order to delineate the terms of the crisis we face today. Such a mapping, or cartographic refrain, should address the following themes as so many interdependent effects of intensive expropriation: in relation to the prison — overcrowding, universalized criminality, extra-institutional observation; in the hospital — the extension of life, the interconnectivity of global disease control and the failing of government support for universal health care; in the factory — automation, downsizing, outsourcing; in educational institutions — the need to keep up with innovation, the transition to knowledge production, the privatization of public interests; in the family — the further atomization of inter-subjective relations, rising divorce rates, absentee parents and the decline of the social welfare system.

In short, the crisis of enclosures is a crisis of capital related to the tendency of the rate of profit to fall and its radical acceleration vis-à-vis the erosion of market regulations, global competition and the dramatic expansion of the financialization sector through hyperbolic fractalization.[65] Such a heightening of contradictions is apparent wherever spiraling poverty is reinforced by the escalating cost of education; where the lack of prison reform mirrors the evaporation of jobs and the need for perpetual retraining; where escalating health problems are exacerbated by the unlimited working-day; where falling wages are further eroded by the extension of the retirement age and reduction of social security benefits; where the factory society is speeded to its death by the dismantling of unions, the institution of right-to-work acts and crowd-sourcing; where public schools cease to serve their democratic function with the institution of limited charter programs, lottery selections, the spread of the voucher system and a general crisis of funding and corporatization; and the nuclear family is dissolved by the exhaustion of contending with the implosion of every last public institution that once supported its continuing viability as a social-form. This is the common horizon of the crisis of enclosures today — a general inability to resist being liquidated and incorporated into the ethos of hyperbolic capitalism, or what Walter Benjamin called the transformation of capitalism into religion — where cultural, familial, educational, and correctional institutions become little more than the remainder of production itself.[66] But what does the crisis of enclosures have to do with Panoptic control — if anything? How are we to think about Panoptic power after the deterritorialization of institutional space, and even after the end of the experience of interiority associated with the modern autonomous subject?

The most readily apparent answer to these pressing questions is that Panopticism is implicated in every form of social organization that relies on the *power of enclosures* to (re)produce the effects of subjectivation, (prison, factory, hospital, school, etc., etc.). However, what Gilles Deleuze could not have foreseen was that Panopticism would return as a power of disclosure rather than enclosure — that it would become an 'all-revealing' apparatus rather than an 'all-seeing' device. However paradoxical such a situation may seem, neo-Panopticism is defined by an ever-expanding field of observational measures at the very moment that the institutional regimentation of bodies is coming to an end. This is how post-institutional observation finally becomes 'the norm' rather than just an exception to the rule. And it is also why 'the norm' is no longer the high watermark of social control. The interpolative processes of subjectivation that codify and perpetuate the idea of a given 'norm' have already been greatly eroded — or, they have been implemented and naturalized to such a degree that singularity has finally become the new locus of desire — for subjectivity and capital alike.

3.7 From Well Disciplined Subjects to Modulated (in)Dividualism: The Death of the Modern Subject and the End of Organic Sociality.

Yet, what is especially hard to comprehend in this transformation is that neo-Panopticism is wholly post-institutional but not at all post-architectural. This conflicted status is the result of a crisis of accounting for the (in)ability of institutions to reproduce well-disciplined subjects and still remain financially viable. Afterall, the cost of sustained ideological and technical interpolation is excessively high as well as unnecessary within the regime of hyperbolic capital because almost any skill-set or social commitment to the ethic of production is likely to be obsolete before a subject even enters the labor force, (or at the very least, such skills will already be out of step with the fluid nature of production and its perpetual transformations). If we follow Foucault's definition of institutional/disciplinary subjects to the point of extreme inversion, then the contradictions of post-institutional subjectivation become much easier to grasp:

> Discipline makes individuals; it is the specific technique of a power that regards individuals both as objects and as instruments of its exercise. It is not a triumphant power, which because of its own excess can pride itself on its omnipotence; it is a modest, suspicious power, which functions as a calculated but permanent economy.[67]

If this is a fair characterization of modern discipline, then post-disciplinary societies, (or societies of control), can be understood as a form of socialization that unmakes individuals through exercised modulation — modulated watching, modulated salaries, modulated emotional states, modulated social mobility, modulated geographic mobility, etc., etc. Control is defined not as a 'modest' power but as a power of intensive incentivizing injunctions; not through the power of 'suspicion' but through subtle forms of contrition; not as a power of pure 'calculations' but as the after-effect of instrumentalized illegality set against anonymous forms of dissent. Affective capital is finally that particular form of power which takes the diminution of effective forms of resistance as its determined goal.

For the first time, neo-capitalism is not just driven by the logic of overcoming its own limits, rather, in its current incarnation, (hyperbolic) capitalism is premised on limiting the possibility of its own overcoming. Intensive subsumption is finally agenda-capital rather than just real or formal capitalism — or, one can say that affective capital combines these monikers inasmuch as it has a real-formal-agenda that trolls for new ways to extrapolate wealth without collapsing the system in its entirety, all the while, working toward the limit of radical antagonism, i.e., destructuration/restructuration.

This new state of affairs constitutes a diagram of control connected with neo-Panopticism to the degree that it shares a number of the same investments — i.e., the co-option of organic feelings, the erosion of organic (cyclical) working relations, the undermining of the organic (extended) family — in short, *the total derision of organic being*. As Deleuze has already noted, in the midst of such a crisis the school is replaced by perpetual re-training, the process of examination by continuous modulation, institutional discipline by the expansion of debtors systems and pharmaceuticals, and the system of enclosures by new forms of judicio-legal-economic and technological exclusivity. The advances in surveillance techniques associated with societies of control actually work to invert the operative efficiency of enclosures: once positioned to keep everyone in, they now function to keep everyone out.

Even the key traits of individualism find themselves displaced by the crisis of enclosed-institutional power where the signature has been replaced by the code, the watchword by the password, face-to-face recognition by bio-metrics, interactions by transactions, etc., etc. In this way, dividuation is not only a form of radical de-socialization but also the sign of a subject divided against his or her own interests — a weak operator set against short-term systems of diminishing rewards based on artificial inflation and "rapid rates of turnover" that are "continuous and without limit."[68] Being granted access to education, information, public transit, health care, security, disaster relief and other primary services is no guarantee that the same permissions will be allowed tomorrow — at least, not without further indulgences.

Control societies are conceived of as being built upon pay-to-play services where the commodity form is largely supplemental to the accumulation of profit.[69] In the final analysis, the economy of Panoptic control is complemented by the universalization of capitalist time and the regulations of audio-visual surveillance in a way that few could have foreseen.[70] Hyper Panopticism is a force of appropriations that enables every economy of social exchange to be subsumed by intensive investments in subjective attributions without protest or derision — or rather, neo-Panopticism and hyperbolic capitalism are mutually determining forces in the hyper-reification of the social sphere. They even signal the end of corporeal sociality vis-à-vis the foreclosure of public space, public services, public discourse, public relations, public politics and even public wars.

Or, to define these ends by their specific means, all of these spaces are slowly becoming commodity-space-forms: public space is replaced by regulatory space and *rentier* space; public services are displaced by pay-to-play actors and private sector interests; public discourse is derided by the dissolution of community functions and hyper-dividuation; public relations are reconfigured by the use of spin doctors, media consultants and event planners; public politics are undermined by scripted inter-actions, focused test groups and the influence of corporate powers; public armies are abandoned in favor of using mercenary forces and contracted service providers — and so on and so on and so on. In this way the *organic bios* is replaced by a *preplanned demos*, where every last space of personal, public and political repose is fully integrated into the circuit of socio-economic exchange. In fact, with hyperbolic capitalism, there is only socio-economic exchange — not a political economy but a social economy — or really an economically-socialized system of exchange that is politicized in even its smallest and most insignificant of determinations.

Consequently, the Deleuzian crisis of enclosures fails out as a paradigm because we now face a crisis of space, civility and public discourse that follows a well-controlled model of expro-priation.[71] To Marx's formulation of ground rent(s) we need to add three new determinations: the ground rent attributable to public space (parking fees, eatery fees, event fees, driving fees, transit fees, etc.), the ground rent of auditory space (cell phone fees, internet fees, protest fees, public gathering fees, recreational fees, etc.), and the ground rent of visual space (filming permits, photography permits, reproduction rights for logos, icons, landmarks, persons, etc.). This is because public-being, public-speaking and public-seeing are the three newest determinations of intensive subsumption outside of an inexplicable spike in all technological rents and/or social-action-fees, (service fees, penalty fees, late fees, etc.). Taken together, these four new forms of expropriation circumscribe the totality of all acts, actions and transactions that can take place in the 'public' sphere — or, they describe the sphere of sociality expunged of its 'publicness' in terms of access, community ownership and usury rights. In a word, these transformations in the social sphere spell the real end of the *commons* defined as communal or community space. Or, to put it somewhat differently, we are here talking about the demise of civil society.

3.8 Affective Capital and the New Diagram of Control: From the Crisis of Enclosures and Foreclosures to the Discursive Power of Unlimited Disclosure.

But what does any of this have to do with revolutions in the mode or production or even revolutions in general? How does the move from post-industrial/multination capitalism to affective/hyperbolic capitalism create the potential for either of these possibilities? Why does idling talk of capitalism devouring itself sound like a story we know only all to well, or like a daydream from a bygone era — and what other outcomes are possible? In short, what are we to make of the potential for post-capitalist societies, alternative forms of social relations and/or the expansion of non-capitalist zones of exchange? How are we to begin thinking our way past these contradictions and antago-nisms — or how might it be possible to construct an arena of productive antagonisms that work to secure the promise of democratic life rather than further eroding its compromised condition?

While hyperbolic capitalism folds the four major modes of social control, (mystic, sovereign, disciplinary and affective), together into new apparatuses of subjectivation, the advent of control societies also inaugurates Marx's final phase of intensive contradictions by making 'the expropriation of the expropriators' a real possibility.[72] Although Hardt and Negri have provided a profound mediation on this crossing in their trilogy about resis-tance as bio-political action, (*Empire*, *Multitude* and *Commonwealth*), we still remain both before and after this revolu-tionary refrain.[73] Before it, because the consolidation of wealth in first world countries has only recently begun to flow from the hands of the many into the hands of the few as part of a post-nationalist, post-corporatist zero sum game.[74] After it, because control societies attempt to combat this social and structural problematic by turning the people against their own self-interest through heightened competition and economic precariousness — everywhere ignoring the rapidity and acceleration of economic crisis, social crisis, educational crisis, environmental crisis, health care crisis, the spreading crisis of mental illness and so on and so forth that has resulted from the intergeneration of capital into every sphere of sociality. In this regard, hyperbolic capital is also a form of dis-associative capital that fosters anti-usefulness, institutionalized outmodedness and inbuilt ex-piration. It is a dis-functional mode of production based on accelerated obsoles-cence, the naturalization of co-dependent life-long usury fees and dis-functionally appropriated social relations of every imaginable kind, (the naturalized indifference of thing-being). Above all else, it is these factors that have brought control societies into existence, and not just as a means of exerting power over the field of sociality, but as a necessary correlative to the invention of new forms of social regulation that are essential to maintaining the regime of hyper-expropriation.

If the *crisis of enclosures* is what allowed Gilles Deleuze to claim that "The operation of markets is now the instrument of social control", then today, it is the *crisis of foreclosures* that serves the same purpose — and not just the foreclosure of homes, but the foreclosure of public spaces, private spaces and all other spaces for thinking outside of the appropriative logic of hyper-bolic capitalism.[75] It is even the (fore)closure of bodily orifices, sutured without leash or tether, by the powers of disclosure, affiliation and improbable connexion that defines social control in the twenty-first century.

Such an absurd state of affairs makes the possibility of resis-tance or revolution seem illegible, or at least untenable — but this has everything to do with how different forms of socio-economic (de)regulation, psychological unease and class stratifi-cation are maintained by the designs of revisionary Panopticism. And yet, neo-Panopticism should not be associated with forms of repression born of institutional command but with a power of *subjectivizing compression* that is co-extensive with the erosion of all institutionally sanctioned authority — a state of affairs that has given free reign to a near omniscient power of unlimited disclosures without institutional motivation, i.e., of creating a state of near permanent observation without clearly defined imperatives. As such, addressing the means and modalities of neo-Panopticism is a way of identifying zones of resistance that make a multitude of revolutionary potentials localizable, and/or, of realizing the possibility of de-subjectivation from the identi-factory-industrial-complex.

3.9 From Global Panopticism to Naturalized Penitentiarism: Control in the Era of Socio-Economic Anomalies and Metastasized Capital.

However, these new conditions also make it necessary to attempt a provisional cartography of how power operates in control societies — the material comport of its mechanisms; the machinations of its modulations; and the indiscreet nature of its periodic interventions. But before new forms of critical and popular resistance can be invented, we must inquire into how variability and nuance are related to subjection and subjectivation; how they work to fortify the processes and procedures that are complimentary to expropriation; and even how they show themselves through the logic of commodity-forms.

Of course, the answer to such an inquiry is no mystery. Control societies rely on nothing less than the attenuated modulation of emotions, performa, profit, access, value, etc., in order to sustain and reproduce the hyperbolic order of expropriation. This shows itself most distinctly in the inversion of the chain of production: where input determines output, where customization maximizes profitability, and where the labor of consumption finally becomes synonymous with the labor of production as the latest technique, (in a long line of techniques), for maximizing economic returns vis-à-vis absolutist co-option. But this is merely its extensive dimension — the contours of a transversal subjectivizing apparatus. Hyperbolic capital also produces subjects that are co-constitutive with the order of production itself; the bi-polarity of its boom bust cycles; the schizo-desires of motivated consumption; the co-dependency of usury fees; the precarity of short-lived use-values; and the depression that accompanies social unusefulness, rising poverty, disproportionate inflation and diminished opportunities for social mobility. This is the *intensive dimension* of hyper capitalism — its *in-bodied* or parasitic aspect — or simply, its indo-colonial operation.

But how exactly does this occur, and under what terms? Is a qualitative understanding of how hyperbolic capitalism produces and reproduces subjects of control in its extensive and intensive determinations even possible? And how does this complex articulation of forms fortify or subvert the fourfold diagram of power that constitutes the neo-Panoptic regime? How do we begin to think of control societies not so much as a new stage of development in disciplinary means but as the anomalous expansion of all former models of control; their total integration; their synergistic stratification; their cartographic interpenetration and so on and so forth. In what ways does the crisis of institutional enclosures end in *wording-enclosure*, i.e., in the world of post-institutional observation? And how has the recent crisis of foreclosures and the expansion of disclosures begun to feel like a foregone conclusion where every last trace of organic being is slowly and systematically eradicated by the subjectivizing processes associated with intensive subsumption?

The simplest retort to such a question is that neo-Panopticism is nothing less than the universalization and multiplication of pre-Panoptic, Panoptic and post-Panoptic means constituted by the fourfold diagram of control — the revelation not only of global Panopticism but of global penitentiarism. But such a sweeping claim tells us very little about the 'totalizing' nature of the fourfold diagram of power today — how it is deployed in concrete terms and how it updates and renews pre-Panoptic and Panoptic models of power that threaten to double over into a nearly autonomic regime of subjectivation. Such an obvious reply doesn't delineate the post-historical condition of techno-cratic power as a series of interpenetrating forces, or how it is defined around optic and even post-optic regimes of control.

Such broad generalizations also avoid providing any articulation of how the Panopticon has become synonymous with an optic-*con* that relies on systems of simulation, virtualization and deification that institute and consolidate the divisions of class power. Consequently, it is these themes that will be examined at length in the following section.

FOURTH MEDITATION

The Fourfold Science of Subjectivation as a System of Apparatuses

Consider, in *Discipline and Punish*, the paradoxical character of what Foucault describes as the subjectivation of the prisoner. The term "subjectivation" carries the paradox itself: *assujetissement* denotes both the becoming of the subject and the process of subjection – one inhabits the figure of autonomy only by becoming subjected to a power, a subjection which implies a radical dependency. For Foucault, this process of subjectivation takes place centrally through the body.[76]

Judith Butler

Power, after investing itself in the body, finds itself exposed to a counter-attack in that same body... But the impression that power weakens and vacillates here is in fact mistaken; power can retreat here, re-organize its forces, invent itself elsewhere . . . and so the battle continues.[77]

Michel Foucault

The body itself has emerged as a legitimate surveillance target because of the immense level of detail and 'truth' about the person it is thought to provide.[78]

Kirstie Ball

4.1 Synopticism and the New Science of Speculating on Subjectivity: Identifactory Fortification, Instrumental Iteration and Hyper-Sensitized Neo-Narcissism.

The first of these fourfold designs of power, the Synopticon, is the dispositif that most decidedly resembles pre-panoptic regimes of control. Defended by the surveillance theorist Thomas Mathiesen as a different way of understanding the diagram of contemporary power, the 'syn'-optic inverts the operations of 'pan'-optic surveillance — it is the gaze of the many fixed on the few — and usually, on figures of prestige.[79] Where sovereign rule once demanded dedicated watching through festival, ceremony and decree, this same orientation toward subjectivation, (one which produces subjects for a king), has been updated by so many forms of *syn*-chronous media consumption. Much like pre-modern forms of Synopticism, the contemporary marriage of power and image privileges certain types of utterances, interactions, body types, dress, postures, etc., etc. However, in opposition to its sovereign and mystical forerunners, electronic Synopticism is more of a distributed power than a ceremonial obligation. At best, we might say that neo-Synopticism is a type of personal accord, or even a means of elevating certain personas to the status of brand names and all-too-plastic commodity-forms, (the worship of thing-likeness). Over time, this kind of imagistic enculturation produces a quasi-metaphysical power of attribution in the popular mind that invites emulation from dedicated watchers.

Which of these variations on Synoptic power is the most compelling form of subjectivation, sovereign or contemporary, is still a 'live' debate in the social sciences. At this juncture, all we can say for sure is that contemporary Synopticism is wholly Foucaultian in being associated with the micro-physics of power and the fourfold designs of neo-Panoptic control. As such, electronic Synopticism is always and everywhere, an apportioned power. It is a regime of soft interpolation which feeds on the desire for identification with a paternal love object at the very moment that all other forms of familial belonging are being dissolved by the spatial and temporal demands of hyperbolic capitalism. It is even a function of what many have termed 'hype-capitalism' — or the new science of speculating on the value of subjectivity.

4.2 The Megalomanized Monad and Synoptic Subjectivation: The Hermeneutic Design of Habituated Potentials, Hyper-Motivated Consumption and Anticipatory Desires.

By compounding its mediated and re-mediated effects, electronic Synopticism works to attune its subjects to systematized watching, sensitized watching and commercial archetypes that 'play well' with viewers while relying on subtle forms of social sorting, (narrowcasting, data mining and feedback loops), that have little to do with the administered power of ages past. As such, the Synoptic effect is synonymous not only with the naturalization of watching as a social practice, but also with the global effects of anti-socialization, where the same kinds of images are returned with increasing efficiency to the same types of viewers, cultures and even nation-states. For the first time we can speak of superstructural, supra-cultural or even transnational forms of (in)dividuation rather than just familial, local and/or national forms of identifactory-belonging.

However, in such a scenario, you don't so much discover a synoptic world *as it discovers you*. After entering into the cartographic assemblages of Synopticism and its various apparatuses of capture, (TiVo, club cards, members privileges, etc., etc.), a subject's future interests will begin to be forecasted well ahead of their current wants; desires will be found before the body begins producing them; and 'the best all possible worlds' will be projected everywhere as a condition of self-same synchronicity — or really, as a catalyst for the intensive designs of advertising proffered as a discipline of premeditated complicity. In this way, the interiority of the modern monad is externalized, megalomanized, and re-inscribed everywhere in the world as its most efficient cause. With the passing of time, the Synoptic effect becomes amplified — atomizing subjects that much more concretely through the continuous co-option of their activities for commercial gain.

Synoptic power is perhaps best exemplified by the insatiable drives of Mr. Smith from The Matrix trilogy, who, after being cut off from communion with the virtual world, feels condemned to an existence of unendurable isolation that doubles over into a cry for self-replication — "more me!" In this way, the desire for liberation from the dominion of the self, (or selves as the case may be), increases in direct proportion to the force of repetition created by the evacuation of organic interactions.

But what is truly unanticipated about our situation today is that this fictionalized situation is reversed — the Synoptic subject is colonized by virtuality through and through as a means of accounting for organic derivations and the potentials they incur (unanticipated interests, disjunctures in consumptive habits, marginal positions within various social networks, etc.). In fact, one could say that Synoptic subjectivation in control societies is circumscribed by a technological dimension, or really, *a kind of technological dementia,* that mistakes organicism for the proliferation of postulated selves within a system of statistical averages. Under this diagram of control, the categorical push toward Synoptic confirmation is heightened by minor deviations in preference that produce the feeling of difference *in kind* without any substantive measure. In turn, these slight deviations in Synoptic socialization tend to function as subjective variations within a sophisticated play of identifactory fortification that undermines any 'encounter' of otherness by reinforcing the habituated potentials associated with motivated and under-motivated consumption. In this recursive loop of subjectivation, the real and the virtual collide as technological retention and instrumental iteration collude against every form of subjective self-invention (re/desubjectivation).

In this way, dividuation and social atomization produce more than just isolation — they are the basis of a radical hermeneutics of self-perception that is overdetermined by commercial forecasting and the systematic exclusion of arbitrary alternatives — or really, by the inclusion of new tendencies as a powerful force of reterritorialization. With the advent of Synopticism, co-option has been transformed into a pro-option — an uncanny moment of attribution accorded to the providence of commercialized subjectivity, (as well as 'alternative' forms of subjectivity). In any or all of its measures, electronic Synopticism is based on alternating signals, AC/DC subjects, binarized subjectivation and strong and weak currents, i.e., on the multiplication of digital modes of recuperation. In the final analysis the Synopti-*con* relies more on commercial co-operation than commercial co-option. In all of its varied forms, Synopticism has come to represent the radial multiplication of a community of one(s), i.e., the production of hyper-sensitized neo-narcissism as the *fait accompli* of the commodified self.

4.3 Synopticism as Spectacular Interpellation: Demography and the Demagoguery of Capital After Debord.

And while the perpetual reinforcement of the self-same worldview is the Synoptic effect par excellence, (the creation of a self-abiding Panopticism), the real crux of Synoptic power is that it individuates as it homogenizes; that it isolates as it brings together; and that it naturalizes the notion that the rights of the watched are without merit while simultaneously fortifying their collective influence. Even though Guy Debord already described this same effect as a by-product of spectacle culture, what he could never have imagined is that images could be routed by demography, and even singularly, in such a way that class subjectivation would rely on reducing irregularities in the reproduction of the social order by making them 'the norm' in a process of hyper-dividuation.[80] Synoptic power achieves this through a subjectivizing spiral of perfected confinement and self-imposed de-socialization — everywhere profiting from a reduction of the multiplicity of being to the fatalism of the one. Synopticism's incontestable goal is to perfect the oroborian subject of virtual de-differentiation — or to sanctify the machinations of self-conformation as a process of self-deformation.

This is achieved when the general production of homogeneity is mistaken for heterogeneity, when dividuals become a stand-in for individuals and when minor eccentricities are interpreted as an emblem of 'the unique'. Synopticism is a form of subjective interpolation that advances as an accumulated effect of self-interest — it is a type of synchronic hailing which is self-initiated and auto-valorized — or simply a co-constituent force in the production of identity circumscribed by double indemnity, (the death of the individual that happens to pay out twofold).

But what is often missing from accounts of Synopticism is that this looping effect also works to atomize class identification because it relies on the destruction of affillial interests outside the self, and by proxy, it also enacts the destructuration of class identity as-such. Or, to put it somewhat differently, Synopticism universalizes the ethos of commercial marketing techniques that valorize affective individualism, while utilizing the effects of technopticism to develop a semi-systemic regime of homogenous subjectivation. Consequently, the marriage of consumerism and Synoptic power — or really their integration into one and the same apparatus — reinforces the production of every inter-polative refrain that opposes anti-capitalist solidarity. Synopticism only leaves minor traces of subculture and counter-culture dis-identification in its wake, and even then, these passing forms of resistance to economic expropriation are instantaneously aestheticized, marketed and integrated into an antagonist process that expands the limits of capitalist rule. Against the absolutism of Synoptic interpolation, counter-culture polemics are little more than a passive interim effect — the sign of a failed politics that doesn't depart from considering hyperbolic capital as a near totalizing horizon that easily subsumes every intervention that explicitly or implicitly identifies with a politics of the 'outside'. It is even the pronounced absence of an outside to capitalist relations that defines the power of the Synoptic apparatus today.

Paradoxically, Synopticism has even entered into a parasitic relation with itself by developing a recursive strategy that takes 'trending' to be an overdetermined loop of auto-valorization that looks to the 'outside', (defined by marketing doublespeak as every form of auto-poetic production external to current market trends), in an effort to redefine the central motifs of *consumption* through the hyperactivity of coordinated cultural forecasting. In other words, the spatial and temporal distance between the periphery and the center has collapsed with the advent of techno-Synoptic dividuation. The Synopticon names a function that was once considered internal to the capitalist regime but which has since been realized in an explicit manner as a new marketing stratagem, i.e., as the hyperbolic co-option of emergent trends, forecasted to an audience of one(s), that is always already immanent to the field of desire. In such a spiral of motivated consumption what circulates at the margins of culture is sold back to the center as 'the new' — and in most cases, as new marginalia. This is the other sense in which the symbolic dimension of contemporary life has begun to collapse — the acceleration of cyclical advertising, (and even of non-cyclical forms of consumerist customization), makes any difference between margin and center imperceptible, not only because the relationship between these temporal and spatial coordinates is highly overdetermined but also because the current pace of production institutes a state of cultural meta-stability where extreme acceleration creates a profound sense of stillness, or a kind of "hummingbird effect" where change can only be detected rather than felt.[81]

4.4. Synopticism as the First Variation on Intensive and Extensive Control: The Rise of Poly-Synchronic Models of Mass Customization and the (auto)Valorization of the Few.

As such, electronic Synopticism represents a profound reversal of the Panoptic diagram of control as well as a striking inversion of monarchical and feudal models of Synoptic power. While the Synoptic gaze of re-mediated existence is just as totalizing as its premodern counterparts — and perhaps even more so for instituting a state of permanent availability — it is especially effective for allowing its subjects to pick their kings, everywhere producing *sovereignty by selection!* Or worse yet, neo-Synopticism is a type of power that fortifies the exercise of sovereign rule over and against its subjects through the automated selection of wish fulfillment experienced as auto-poetic intimations. In such a scenario the king really does give his subjects what they want by holding court with the big Other of consumerist prophecy — aligning today's wants with the sensibilities of the past and a calculated number of possible futures.

The transcendent designs of Synoptic power are a consequence of accounting for the predestination of desire through advanced techniques of solicitation, inference and deduction — or really, of identifying the potential for an (in)dividual's susceptibility to fads, iterations, product savings, cross-marketing promotions, cultural associations, group discounts, point-of-purchase bonuses and even the sheer pleasure of consumption itself. It is a kind of subjectivation *in-suti* that is propagated through an exponential increase in the totality of available information on consumptive trends, i.e., the obscene projection of endless forms of self-aggrandizement produced through generative suggestions and data tracking. While Synoptic power was only ever conceived of as the periphery watching the center — where the center cannot (always) gaze upon the totality of its given subjects — today's poly-synchronic networks can and do look back on individual subjects, (dividuated subjects), in order to marshal the powers of the body toward projected desires, (hyper-motivated consumption).

Paradoxically, this is achieved by calculating and cataloging the accumulated effect of consumptive trajectories, their compounded inter-circuitous connections and their culture wave patterns vis-à-vis the new science of inferrogatory telematics. David Lyon has presented us with a short genealogy of how the diagram of control is associated with sovereign societies, disciplinary societies and societies of control in relation to corporeal (in)dividuation by highlighting the aesthetic and commercial dimension of (neo)Synoptic control:

> If the premodern concern was with how a body should *live*, and modernity was dominated by the question of how a body is *known* (which, of course, lies behind surveillance in many of its forms), late- or postmodern culture shifts the question to how the body looks. There is an apparent shift from the analytic to the aesthetic.[82]

Or, we could amend this last statement to say the premodern/modern/postmodern divide is really split between a diagram of power that moves from the symbolic to the analytic to the aesthetic. And while this journey from the love of the sovereign (symbolic power) to the love of inspection (analytic power) to the love of looking (aesthetic power) seems to be an adequate expression of where we are today, electronic Synopticism really joins these three forms of control into one and the same act as a superadded effect. Universalized scopophelia is even a type of heightened sovereignty — where inspection is both the act of the sovereign toward his/her imagined subjects (symbolic power) *and* the perspective of subjects who remain transfixed on the immaterial power of tele-presence (aesthetic power), distributed and qualified as it is, by dividuated marketing/marking techniques (analytic power). In this recursive loop, looking and being looked at both concretize the power of market forces by increasing one's sense of being catered too — the projection of a market designed-for-one married to the auto-valorization of the few. Regrettably, this tri-part configuration of self-sanctification is anything but the exercise of sovereign individualism. In fact, *it is the exact opposite.*

Synopticism represents the multiplication of fragmented and partial subjects divided not by self-interest, but by being interested in developing 'a sense of self'; it is not a regime of organic subjects but of wholly saturated subjects; it doesn't build relational subjects but only an intra and/or infra-relationality of the self with the self. However, in acknowledging that this is indeed the case, neither Mathesian nor Lyon ever defended the thesis that Synoptic pleasure has replaced Panoptic power. Quite to the contrary, they concur that Panopticism has found an infinite number of new applications alongside the assemblage of the electronic Synopticon. If anything, they are mutually reinforcing powers — the return of pre-modern forms of emulation and secular deification positioned within the Enlightenment design of partitioned and conditioned watching — a Panopticizing Synopticon joined to a Synopticizing Panopticon! In this way, the 'crisis of enclosures' is superseded by an enclosed sense of self where institutional control becomes superfluous in the aftermath of institutionalized subjectivity. As such, *the first variation on intensive and extensive modulation ascribed to revisionary Panopticism* can be triangulated along the following lines: the love of emulation (sovereignty) buoyed by forms of self-immolation (self-defacement) and the love of looking (scopophelic over-identification) sutured to two way channels of self-inspection, i.e., partitioned televisual subjectivation concretized by consumerist divination.

4.5 Banopticism and the New Science of Speculative Restrictions: Coordinated Apparatuses of Surveillance, Post-Statist Models of Judico-Legal Intervention and Instrumentalized Techniques of Suspicion.

In contrast to Panopticism (the few watching the many), or Synopticism (the many watching the few), Banopticism has to do with the many watching the many — or the de-differentiation of national and transnational, private and public, and professional and casual modes of surveillance. The Ban-optic diagram of control is largely a delocalized, proactive and strategic mode of intervention, while the Pan-optic is centralized, reactive and scrutinizing, and the Syn-optic is repetitive, selective and fluid. The Banoptic doesn't represent a unified strategy but networked forms of policing: technological, biological, legal, etc. Didier Bigo, the central theorist of Banoptic power, has noted that Banopticism is not something like "a panopticon transposed to a global level" but that 'the ban' "both signifies the exclusion enacted by the community and serves as the insignia of *sovereignty* (my emphasis). It is what is excluded from sovereignty on high as exception to the rule and what is excluded from below as discrimination, rejection, repulsion and banishment."[83] Unlike the extreme legibility of the ban associated with totalitarianism, the operation of the Ban-optic is not so much a power of announced prohibition(s) as it is a means of tracking social and corporeal inscriptions through a wide variety of policing techniques. The Banoptic is more of a coordinated power of prevention than an enforced measure of explicit restrictions. Or, to be a bit more concise, the Banoptic represents a radical hermeneutics of suspicion circumscribed by a post-statist diagram of power.

4.6 Interrogating the Banoptic Apparatus: Redefining legality, Incrimination and Conspiratory Intimations in the Field of Social Exchange.

If there is a singular trait that separates the Banoptic from the Panoptic (self-regulating power) and the Synoptic (self-sanctifying power), it would have to be that it is a paradigm of control focused on identifying the potential for criminal activity through the qualification of pragmatico-statistical predestination (self-incriminating power). But how is this achieved — and toward what end(s)? Is Banopticism an adjudicated power, a diminutive power or a power of aversion — or even a pre-operative series of indicators? Is 'the ban' now something that proceeds the moment of illegality rather than defining the terms and conditions of prohibited activities? Are we facing the production of an institutionalized *pre-Banoptics* that is not so much concerned with the violation of the law but the illegality of events — of governance 'about' incrimination and recriminations rather that criminal activities — or of turning the subject into a thingly figure of criminality, i.e., it-criminalization?

Or, to put it somewhat differently, is the ban-*optic* focused on what conspires rather than what transpires? Is it something like a new diagram of virtual positions and axiomatic transpositions that are mobilized against (in)dividuals in order to produce judico-legal impositions? And if so, what are the terms that allow us to negotiate the Banoptic apparatus? Is Banopticism simply utilitarian (protectionist), totalitarian (demonstrative) or communitarian (faux neo-liberal universalism)? Or worse yet, is the Banopti-*con* simply a consequence of how modernity has come to signify the unlimited expansion of economic, scientific and political catastrophes? Such questions require a more sweeping description of Banoptic techniques and procedures as well as their deployment over and against the body socius. Not only do we need to triangulate Banopticism's 'optic' capacities and techniques, but it is also crucial to touch upon its archio-technostructural mechanisms, i.e., its function as a 'Ban'-opticon.

4.7 Banopticism as an Alliance Power: The Advent of Post-Liberal Forms of Governance Based on Corporeal Tracking, Territorial Redistricting and Transversal Policing Agencies.

If we were to sum up the operative traits of Banopticism, it would be worth noting that the Ban-optic is not unlike other contemporary modes of surveillance and control in being an assemblage power. However, in sharp contrast to the hierarchical and semi-hierarchical relations internal to Panopticism and Synopticism, power is distributed though the Banoptic apparatus in a more oblique and enigmatic manner. On the whole, it is far less transparent, functioning like a mitigated hierarchy of sorts, or an interlocking system of semi-hegemonic actors. Banopticism is by and large mobile; judging 'at risk' zones, groups and individuals; developing new forms and categories of policing; cross-networking between private agencies and government institutions to build data-doubles of every action and infraction in the social field — all the while, moving surveillance toward a paradigm of (in)dividuation, polarization and virtuality. Banopticism expands its exegesis over the field of sociability by creating expanded cartographies of 'hot' zones where conflicts can be anticipated and subverted before they happen. As a paradigm of policing, the Banoptic is premised on the effectivity of producing and acting on foreknowledge 'about' criminal activities. Banoptic power is both *sovereign* in its deployment and *exceptional* in its exercise. At best, it can be characterized as a system of preventative measures — at worst, as a power of pre-judgment, extreme prejudice and errant command.

After Synopticism, the Ban-optic marks the second return of pre-modern power placed under the sign of neo-sovereign practices of governmentality, (albeit a Schmittian post-secular definition of sovereignty).[84] In many ways, Banopticism resembles a form of inverted totalitarianism, where the universality of protectionism is deployed through a doctrine of pre-emptive actions, military strikes and undeclared wars. It is the unilateral will to act first among an uneasy alliance of coordinated, and sometimes not so coordinated powers — or something like a permissive form of fascist rule, (if this isn't too much of an oxymoron)!

The Banoptic is comparable to articulating a type of neo-Orwellian complex that is exercised through the intuitions and imperatives of fragmented extra-legal policing agencies. Or, to put it in contemporary cinematic terms, the exercise of Ban-optic power increasingly resembles the fictional premise of Steven Spielberg's 2002 movie *Minority Report*. However, instead of relying on the psychic visions of semi-lucid pre-cogs to eliminate criminal activity, Banopticism is that peculiar form of instrumental reason that is triangulated between post-cognitive observers and technological means, i.e., through the thorough-going co-ordination of data tracking programs.

In judico-legal terms, Banopticism consists of the radical decriminalization of extra-legal actors (mercenaries), extradition policies (post-national security) and detainments camps (the routinization of totalitarian practices) posited as the only possible means of maintaining an abiding, and wholly illusionary, sense of peace. These are the structures which divide and recombine in the diagram of control associated with Banopticism, its manifold procedures, its multiplicitous points of command and its proliferating jurisdictions. As such, Banopticism represents an alliance power of shifting determinations that attend the process of subjectivation through judico-legal registration(s), politico-geographical re-districting and transversal policing directives.

4.8 Banopticism as the Second Variation on Intensive and Extensive Control: The Deployment of Neo-Sovereign Power, Rhizomatic Discipline and the Naturalization of the 'State of Exception' in Constitutional Democracies.

Yet, the most important factor in defining the deployment of Banoptic power in its intensive and extensive determinations has barely been touched upon outside of a general description of its features. Understanding the broader social and political implications of Banopticism means seeing its core traits and the deification/reification of its merits as co-extensive with the naturalization of the 'state of exception' in western democracies — or the implementation of what Giorgio Agamben calls constitutional dictatorship.[85] Banoptic rule goes against the principles of democratic life not only by erasing due process, eliminating privacy, and subverting any reliable system of checks and balances, but also by ushering in the end of modern liberalism defined as the separation of institutional powers. This is because the diagram of 'the ban' is one in which every power comes together: church and state, corporations and state, state and state, state and supra or extra-statists powers, etc., etc. It is the consummate exercise of disciplinary mechanisms where the whole is *more than* just the sum of its parts. In this way the citizen never faces the state proper but only a series of statist positions, policing practices and interventionist agencies.

In strictly Marxian terms, Ban-optimism represents something like the unlimited extension of a kind of judico-legal overdetermination. Or, following Bigo's definition, we could say that the Banopti-*con* represents a concentrated attempt to strike at the "structural logic" of violence — an instance of postmodern (il)legality aimed at upending the super-structural roots of conflict by "channeling flows", "controlling movement", and "managing at a distance".[86] In this regard, the Banopticon is nothing less than the naturalization of a new form of rhizomatic discipline. But how is all of this achieved — how is liberal society and civic responsibility replaced by a new diagram of control that reconfigures the designs of Panopticism? How is the power of the many folded into a power of surveillance that resembles the power of the one, the total, the 'all-seeing' eye, i.e., the gaze of Panoptic perceptivity?

If anything, Banoptic power has come into existence as a means of surveilling the populations it was meant to protect. It is the nexus effect of intermingling commercial interests with expanded governmental control, where the supposed 'necessity' of overturning civil rights is achieved through the intensive rhetoric of (in)security and the extensive expansion of technological means. Or, to put this change in the diagram of control in more general terms, Banopticism is that particular form of power which denotes the intensification of internal security and the extensive intertwining of transnational and supra-national actors. This constitutes *a second variation on the theme of intensive and extensive (neo)Panopticism after the return of the Synopticon*. It is also the second major reconfiguration of surveillance towards privatization and global forms of subjectivation that rely on a mercenary logic of profitability aimed at securing the seamless reproduction of the social order through extra-legal means.

4.9 Bio-opticism as the New Science of Measuring Biological Forms: On the Uses and Abuses of Indentifactory Infomatics.

The Bio-optic, or the transformation of vision into a new form of bio-power, is probably the least theorized model of revisionary Panopticism. Here I will be using the term Bio-opticism in conjunction with the work of David Lyon, Mark Poster and Gary T. Marx on the themes of electronic Panopticism, super Panopticism and hyper-Panopticism because these three cartographies of social control attempt to confront the question of governmentality and archio-discipline head on. In counter-distinction to Synopticism and Banopticism, the Bio-optic apparatus is the only form of Panopticism that attempts to literally colonize the body: to pass through the body unencumbered; and even to secure a physiological profile of the body and its determinations for the activity of governance. In this regard, the diagram of control associated with Bio-opticism is closer than Synopticism or Banopticism to Bentham's original motives in being a wholly body-oriented paradigm. However, in counter-distinction to Panopticism, who's aim was to 'train' and 'correct' subjects, Bio-opticism is a system of techniques that tends to produce hysterical subjects by always operating in excess of corporeal visibility.

The most well know instance of Bio-opticism is the new science of measuring biological forms known as bio-metricism. This particular model of Bio-optic surveillance continues to expand its catalog of identifactory means vis-à-vis iris scans, facial recognition patterns, x-rays, fluid tests, voice analysis, DNA verification, hand measurements and every other form of documenting the body and its various secretions. Bio-opticism is finally flesh made information — a disciplinary corporeal infomatics. But why is this inexplicable shift in surveillance techniques associated with hyperbolic forms of Panopticism? Why posit the presence of architectural power as complimentary to, or co-extensive with, disciplinary methods for investigating the architecture(s) of the body? Why consider the architectonic alongside the organic; or take social physics to be a question of treating the physique; or redefine the body-in-transit as an object of discrete dissections, virtual vivisections and architectural intersections? Why correlate the notion of indo-colonization with physical *rather than* psychic sublimation; or with judico-legal (re)framing *rather than* enforced policing; or with systems of bio-capture *rather than* telematic screening — especially in relation to the designs of archio-discipline?

Other than the fact these are all mutually determining forces, (where the same architectural arrangements that support optical inspection also function as a means of channeling the body for physical inspection), it is important to place the micro-physics of architectural power and subjectivation under the same rubric of investigation because the digital gaze has finally become that much more Panoptic, not for just seeing you, *but for seeing into you*. That is what draws inspection and vision into a relation with bio-power that moves from discipline to control — from Panopticism to neo-Panopticism — or to Bio-opticism unbound.

4.10 Bio-opticism and the Automatic Functioning of Power: Sub-atomizing Subjectivation as a Dispositif of Hyper-Credentialism, Anticipatory Conformity and Radical Inclusivity.

More than any other trait, to speak of an 'electric Panopticon' is to understand Bio-optics as part of the unending demand for 'credentialism'.[87] As David Lyon has noted, it is the most recent development to 'destroy the certainty of alternative powers' — to know that you are always known, watched and surveilled through and through — with or without natural or legal limit. Under this new model of (bio)surveillance the automatic functioning of power becomes a "calculated technology of subjection" that includes intensified watching in the workplace, intensified categorization in the marketplace, intensified documentation at check points, intensified searches at places of passage and travel, and intensified record keeping of every imaginable kind.[88] In this way the electronic Panopticon surpasses its eighteenth century progenitor by creating the conditions for totalized inclusiveness and 'anticipatory conformity' — not to mention the "radical *(sub)*atomization (my prefix)" of subjective experience.[89]

As a form of Bio-opticism, the electronic Panopticon doesn't universalize fear — it naturalizes it — and it does so at the level of fibrous matter. It represents the end of carceral society and the beginning of a hyperactive 'dialectics of control' constituted by precepts and affects — or really, by stratagems that can be best described as preconscious forms of interpellation.[90] As such, it is important to note that electronic Panopticism is addressed to the bios as a series of post-Althussierian techniques, i.e., as a form of hailing that never need speak the name of a subject nor indicate the mark of a denatured relationship between any *body* in particular and certainly not 'the social body' in general.[91] In fact, electronic Panopticism collapses the second of these two designations into the first, allowing us to speak of a hyper-socialized but radically isolated body whose main forms of subjectivation issue from a process of enterterpellation rather than interpellation (i.e., of concrete psychological and pharmacological colonization rather than (un)conscious forms of social accommodation).[92]

But how do we understand such a change of Panoptic means — or what is the difference between Panopticism and electric/super/hyper Panopticism — especially as a dispositif of Bio-optic control? What are its injunctions and disjunctions; its displays of power and its concealed operations; its duplicitous motivations and its unanticipated departures?

4.11 Bio-opticism as the Concretization of Super Panopticism: Control as a New Language Game Based on Systematic Record Keeping and the Complex Manipulation of Symbols (Semio-Capital).

Here, many answers are possible. In the Panoptic penitentiary individuals try to conceal their actions while in super Panoptic regimes (in)dividuals actively choose to send messages to their watchers. In eighteenth century Panopticism, the act of profiling subjects was determined by a need to accumulate only the most pertinent information, while the rise of super Panopticism brings with it the possibility of an "infinite dossier" — the capture and release of unlimited and unrestricted data of all kinds.[93] Where Bentham's Panoptic program attempted to totalize a discrete field of power relations, the super Panopticon represents a regime of totalized surveillance that is constituted by "systematic record keeping" and the "complex manipulation of symbols".[94]

Mark Poster has even gone so far as to define super Panopticism as "a new language situation" that inverts Bentham's Panoptic/disciplinary economy as well as the eighteenth conception of political economy.[95] This paradoxical turnabout occurs because the flow of information in knowledge-based economies becomes coordinated in its restrictions at the very moment that the energy required for its reproduction falls to nil. This unquantifiable relation to exchange-value may be thought of as post-economic to the degree that it requires a diminishing input of hard energy to sustain the labor of repro-duction. Such an unprecedented mutation in the attribution of 'value' turns the rationalist ethos of deterministic models of political economy upside down, making categories like necessary labor and surplus labor somewhat obsolete — or at least, unquantifiable. And yet, this same trend finds itself offset by an exponential increase in the time required for the development, co-ordination and integration of disparate modes of intellectual production — creating a culture of near endless updates, compat-ibility issues and maintenance services.

This crisis of value around datatization and the information economy makes super Panopticism the last possible means of sanctifying the unlimited expansion of capitalist time and control, not only by making discipline the norm, but by making it contiguous with species-being, (the rise of homo-vigilare). It is even the principle presupposition that has allowed cultures of immaterial (re)production and motivated consumption to triumph over societies of hard production and moderate consumption. Unlike other techniques of Panoptic subjection, super Panopticism's profitability depends not only on the repro-duction of 'perfected' subjects of discipline to carry out the unending task of self-replication (hyperbolic dead labor) — but also on creating a regime of unceasing and ever-accelerating labor processes that make the idea of 'control' seem ironic, or even superfluous. Afterall, who can speak of the need for increasing control in an economy of exhaustion, expiration and overstimulation? Who can defend the need for resistance in a subjectivizing economy without confronting a series of immanent contradictions?

In such a scenario the acute attenuation of labor techniques is qualified by hyper-intensive forms of inspection because labor and Panopticism are mutually determined and mutually determining forces in generating surplus value, (as well as a sign of the crisis around profit, production and lived-time — or really, the 'value' of the time-of-life). But in order to understand an economy where LTV (life-time-value) has become the primary objective of labor processes, it is finally necessary to draw out a larger picture of the history of production itself, its topological shifts, synchronic moments, diachronic unfoldings and so on and so forth.[96]

In socio-economic terms, the pre-capitalist world of work was largely cyclical in nature, tending to rely on the organic life of usable goods and services. Pre-synthetic and pre-industrial production tended to have a short shelf-life that was well integrated into the bio-cycle with few undesirable by-products. By contrast, modernization consisted of regimented, discontinuous and atomized forms of production based on the desire for durable goods and personalized services. During this period of production (formal subsumption) the cyclical nature of labor was jettisoned in favor of retaining the 'natural' working day — or by making the 'working day' into a post-seasonal regime of laboring processes that can serve up the same kinds of products year-round. However, in the move from the formal subsumption of labor by capital (industrialization) to the real subsumption of life by post-industrial production, neo-capitalism began to exceed the fixed terms of political economy by instituting a world of continuous labor and planned obsolescence based on immaterial goods and automated services.[97] In such a scenario the designs of organic production are married to the ethos of industrialization, allowing durable and/or technological goods to acquire a shorter and shorter shelf-life through planned obsolescence. This transformation in the mode of production retains the idea of cyclical expiration as being an essential element in the manufacture of industrial and synthetic goods, even becoming the defining motive for perpetual innovation today.

And yet, all three of these previous phases of 'development' are beginning to be replaced by the designs of affective labor which is not only a continuous means of control but also a wholly over-determined regime of production that strives to overcome every limit-event in the logic of profitability. Affective labor and intensive subsumption is subjectivizing at every level of (social) exchange — requiring both the most profound commitment of belief in its organizational capacities and the becoming-machinic of social reproduction. Affective capital is a hyper-accelerated and programmatic cycle of near instantaneous obsolescence, that is itself, based on the wild proliferation of systemic incompatibility issues — all of which require an illimitable number of service contracts, access codes, updates, protection plans, extended warranty guarantees and limited liability clauses in order to function as an economy at all. In other words, the profitability of decay, depreciation and contamination are now central to maintaining the illusions of a 'growth' economy! In such a regime of production, the bio-cycle of the organic working day, the durability of industrial goods and the forms of planned obsolescence that are associated with technological ex-piration have been jettisoned in favor of a subjectivizing economy based on the radical expropriation of life (time), land (resources) and liberty (democratic freedoms) without recompense.

In direct opposition to pre-modern, modern and postmodern forms of political economy, (or formal, real and intensive subsumption), labor and value are now largely generated before and after production. New commodity forms are predominantly a by-product of intensive development and extensive ownership services, where use value has little or no relation to the material goods from which it is composed. As a consequence, the radical extension of working time is necessary just to maintain the pace of (re)production, (pre)planned generational iterations, information migration and (post-warranty) repairs. This new regime of capitalist development is not only defined by the extension of the working day, it is also circumscribed by the subsumption of subjectivity or 'emotional branding' — where the subject of consumption is no longer just the producer or consumer of commodity-forms. Instead, hyperbolic subsumption means that every social relation is now open to the terms and conditions of commodity logic without reserve. As hard as it is to imagine, the worker is no longer the subject of labor, rather, the *worker now becomes this labor*. As Hardt and Negri pointed out more than a decade ago, intellectual and affective labor takes on an ontological dimension — even becoming the ontology of social relations today.[98]

Within such a paradigm leisure time is increasingly undesirable; heightened competition and precarious profitability overdetermine the need and desire for an unlimited working day; hobbies and side interests find themselves displaced by corrective measures for perfected integration into the social fabric through corporate retreats, motivational counseling and 'life' coaches; familial relations, community activities and hobbies are seen as tertiary activities at best, occupying a sporadic semi-recreational function; language and emotional relations are permeated throughout by the terms and conditions of commodity-objectification; and any effort at self-improvement and education becomes something of a liability if not directly related to improving job security. In the moment of intensive subsumption, capitalist time is both universal and universally 'valued' — often to the near exclusion of every other form of social congress.

This is important for understanding the rise of super Panopticism inasmuch as it is the name for maximizing the (in)efficiency of production — or really the time of pre- and post-production — the two regimes of *labor without limit*. Considered as part of the will toward Bio-opticism, super Panopticism works not just to create the conditions of automation and atomization, but also the naturalized reproduction of automaton consciousness, i.e., the production of perfected and unceasing laborers — or of labor time without a qualifiable remainder.

4.12 Bio-opticism as the Third Variation on Intensive and Extensive Control: Corporeal Data Mining, Obligatory Participation and Totalized Observation as New Forms of Bio-Power.

In this sense indo-colonization is synonymous with the observational directives associated with neo-Panopticism. This has occurred not only because of the dramatic increase in the searching and sorting speed of computational devices, but also because every form of categorization and analogic association feels increasingly arbitrary if not wholly indefensible. Mark Poster describes the symbolic relation engendered by technological encoding as largely valueless because database information is always contextually *underdetermined*. Computational schematization and inter-referential (inferrogatory) sequencing is by and large, a system of registration marks that lacks any evidence of subjective commitment or understanding — not to mention the problems that adhere to attribution, indexicality and the fraternity of signs. As Poster has noted:

A database arranges information in rigidly defined categories or fields. When viewed on a computer monitor or printed out on paper each field is a column and each record a row. Each field contains a limited number of spaces and if the field is for dates or numbers, entries in it are even more limited in their form. Speed and efficiency of the databases varies directly with the fixity of the form in which information appears in it. A database might consist of the following fields: an individual's first and last name, social security number, street address, city, state, zip code, phone number, age, sex, race, unpaid parking violations, x-rated video cassettes rented, subscriptions to communist periodicals. The agency that collects the information in this database constitutes individuals according to these parameters.

Many databases are roughly adequate in relation to the phenomena they signify. As long as the field for the last name has enough spaces for the charters it does not reduce at all the people's names. At the other extreme of fields in databases is 'subscriptions to communist periodicals'. Here the category itself is politically charged. But the way data is entered into the field illustrates well the discursive function of the databases. The name of the journal might be entered into the field but this is less efficient than entering numbers or values for different journals. There might be summary values, for instance 1 to 4, with 4 indicating the most subversive. At this point everything depends on how actual journals receive specific values. *Mother Jones* might be given a 2 and *The New York Review of Books* might be given a 1. In any case, although the relation between journal and value is arbitrary, the number in the field of the database contains no ambiguity. In cases where journals have not been precoded, the value entered in the field is still more arbitrary since it will vary with the person performing the data entry.

The example indicates that the structure or grammar of the database *creates* relationships among pieces of information that *do not exist in those relationships outside of the database* (my emphasis). In this sense databases constitute individuals by manipulating relationships between bits of information. But anyone may scribble away or type this kind of information. What gives databases their effectiveness is not only their non-ambiguous grammatical structure but also their electronic coding and computerized storage. In electronic form data can be stored and searched with breathtaking rapidity, millions of records a second, practically at the speed of light. In our example above the entire population of the United States can be sorted to search for subscribers to *The New York Review of Books* and this information can be transmitted anywhere in the world in a few seconds. If fingerprints and photographic images of individuals are added as fields in a database, as they are currently in police computers, the power of the database to specify individuals becomes clear.[99]

In no uncertain terms, this describes the new and expanding set of Power/Knowledge relations that accompany the diagram of control associated with super/electronic/hyper Panopticism.

But why does this form of technocratic Panopticism need a Bio-optic counterpart? What sustains the driving fascination with providing clearer regimes of identification beyond light and material inscriptions, or the photo and the fingerprint respectively? What is motivating the need to actually penetrate the body for hidden information — to probe beneath its membranes and into its orifices for concealed regimes of data? How much more information can really be provided by 'advanced' screening methods and 'advanced' interrogation techniques? And how are either of these new means of handling the body an 'advancement' over previous methods while there remains an intensive and extensive interest in insignia's *and* signatures; impressions *and* inscriptions; DNA verification *and* background information? A qualitative move forward should find one of these cartographies of identification holding a place of privilege over the other rather than just presenting us with a redoubling of forces — and yet, *this is not the case today.*

But why and how did this paradoxical situation become the status quo of contemporary surveillance? Is it because the validity of databases depends on identifying an accurate trace of the subject in question, however impractical and obtuse the means of capture? Or, is it because the collection and correlation of corporeal data offers us the hope of providing an incontestable picture of local orientation and motive? Or, is it because the idea of history without progress everywhere calls for a doubled and redoubled sense of security that can only be pursued through the unrestrained expansion of instrumental forms of observation?

Irrespective of which of the above premises sounds the most plausible, it has become increasingly clear that every form of conjecture associated with data-veillance remains troubled by the classic problem of needing to prove causation. Subjectivity isn't reducible to social patterning in much the same way that live polling trends tend to overlook the event of reflective consciousness. Subjectivity is always in excess of its traces and associations; its inputs and outputs; its motives and designs — it is always something *more than and less than* its categorical deter-minations — coming too late to be perceived correctly in 'the moment' and too early to be anticipated retroactively.

Such contradictions make the paranoiac imaginary associated with super-Panopticism into a viscous circle of ever greater cataloging and verification. In such a chiasmic feedback loop the first moment of interlocution (supposedly) certifies the authen-ticity of all that follows, while what follows is seen as validating the premise of the original inquiry in a process that can only be described as a turn-style logic of social appropriation motivated by the unlimited quest to 'picture' a subject and the totality of his/her actions, i.e., to literally make subjection and subjecti-vation a process of total visibility.[100] That is what makes Bio-optics and super-Panopticism the site of bio-power today.[101] The Bio-optic represents the intensification of locating subjects in space and time while electric/super/hyper-Panopticism signals the extensive interlocution of their interests, hobbies, desires, etc. In other words, along with Synopticism and Banopticism, *Bio-opticism is the third great mutually conditioning force of neo-Panoptic interpolation.* Bio-opticism qualifies the deployment of neo-Panoptic power in the social field while making the bios into a function of infra- and supra-visibility.

In summation, Bio-opticism, Banopticism and Synopticism all extend the subjectivizing dimension of Panopticism from architectures of control to architectures of the body as part of an ever expanding set of sovereign judicio-legal imperatives.

4.13 (Pan)Acousticism and the New Science of Audio-Visual Monitoring: Subjectivation and the Power of the Sound-(Movement)-Image in Control Societies.

But even with the near perfected deployment of optic power(s) in the social field a crucial fourth component is still missing — *the Acousticon.* Of course, the obvious objection to adding one more fold in the contemporary design of Panoptic power comes about because this is not an optic power but an auditory power, i.e., the power of the few to hear the many. For the large majority of surveillance theorists, the Acousticon has no proper place in any discussion about optics and control, and least of all, in the hyper-visible regime of observation associated with contemporary Panopticism. At best, the Acousticon has been seen as tangential to such concerns — or as something of a supplement to observa-tional/obser-*vocational* techniques.

In refuting these entrenched positions, it is necessary to highlight two important aspects of the relationship between vision and sound within the history of Panopticism. First off, it is crucial to remember that later editions of the Panopticon did include the monitoring of inmate chatter. *Panopticism is, and has always been, the dream of total surveillance.* Second, at the close of the twentieth century, vision appears to be irrevocably interwoven with sound in a way that was unimaginable in ages past. Be it through the i-phone, Skpe or audio-visual messaging, sound is now everywhere sutured to the production of (moving) images — making auditory transmissions an integral part of the visual spectrum. Sound waves have even been given visual representation through surveillance amplification, de-scrambling devices and noise analysis filters. As a consequence, the world of auditory communication can now be visualized, graphed, decoded, simulated, separated and transformed into infomatics. These two factors make the development of the Acousticon something that comes both before and after the Panoptic penitentiary — before it, as an imaginative projection of seventeenth century absolutism, (Pan-Acousticism), and after it, as a rather recent superadded effect (electronic Pan-Acousticism). As such, acoustic observation is anything but a secondary or marginal technique within the Panoptic apparatus.

4.14 The Four Dimensions of Panacousticism: Stratospheric, Geographic, Local and Personal.

If we were to draw out a diagram of (pan)Acousticism, or to articulate its place within the designs of revisionary Panopticism, then its various apparatuses of capture would have to be placed alongside every other model of surveillance aimed at cataloging the body and its movements. Perhaps best thought of as various levels of strata, the least of these, or at least the furthest removed, would be satellite surveillance. Next would be eye-in-the-sky drones, which would then be followed by all forms of ground surveillance, and finally, by the addition of every type of handheld audio-visual device. While each of these stratospheric, geographic, local and personal surveillance devices has an audio-visual capacity particular to its own constitution, it is helpful to think of this dynamic cartography in relation to the fourfold diagram of Panoptic power and its concentrated effects.

In this way, not only have Bentham's late designs been realized in a manner that exceeds the piped rigging of two-way echo cambers, but the electronic Acousticon returns us to the absolutist imaginary of seventeenth century power by merging the 'all hearing machine' with the 'all seeing apparatus'. By any measure, the techno-Acousticon is an unparalleled vision, realized through the disciplinary power of teleographic infomatics and cartographic triangulation. It is a power of electromagnetic interlocution unmatched in both its speed and observational efficacy.

And yet, in many ways, the universal disavowal of its viral effects is what prevents western culture from realizing that it may be tumbling backwards through time to sovereign regimes of governance; to neo-feudal economic relations and finally; even to neo-baroque systems of social control. Or worst yet, the real symbolic value of Pan-Acousticism may be the evacuation of the symbolic order tout court — the diminution of the distance between the self and the big Other — or the irrevocable loss of a temporal and spatial respite from watching and listening devices, i.e., the gaze of omnipresent perceptivity. To place this same disjuncture in strictly humanist terms would mean seeing the electronic Acousticon as an accomplice to the death of modern autonomy and even its total derision in postmodern society. With the rise of neo-Acousticism the imaginary space of an unobserved self vanishes, privacy becomes a thing of the past and every form of anonymous action is interpreted as a new form of criminality.[102] But how can we account for this kind of transformation of the public sphere as well as the neglect of Acousticism as a paradigm of surveillance that is directly implicated in the analysis of contemporary audio-visual technologies? — not to mention the return of Panacousticism as a system of disciplinary techniques?

4.15 Panacousticism as a Repressed Figure of the Political Imaginary: Hyper-Surveillance, the End of Anonymity and the Naturalization of Post-Democratic Life.

First of all, the Acousticon is the fanciful precursor to Bentham's project, yet it is ubiquitously absent from most of the discussions of Panoptic power in continental philosophy, including Foucault's. Second, contemporary surveillance studies almost always avoid it as a topic of merit, even when the discussion revolves around understanding what an audio-visual apparatus is and what it purports to do. Third, the Acousticon remains the repressed figure of pre-Enlightenment policing methods because the only thing more upsetting than having fallen prey to universalized (neo)Panopticism more than two centuries after its failed implementation is to have been subsumed by the absolutist diagram of control associated with colonial and monarchical power. Finally, and perhaps the most damning of the indictments presented here, is having witnessed the fall of the modern autonomous subject within a single generation — or to have realized it was a complete fallacy to begin with, where each successive stage of capitalist development demanded tighter and tighter restrictions on the experience of lived-space, movement, observation and anonymity — until the very notion of subjective autonomy simply collapsed under the weight of its own contradictions.

Regrettably, the deployment of audio-visual technologies represents the latest development in an intensive and extensive genealogy of subjectivation that issues from Panoptic devices. As such, the advent of the electronic Acousticon not only undermines our picture of unreserved participation in public and private discourse, but in the U.S. it takes on a decidedly post-democratic twist with the passage of the neo-Orwellian injunction known as the 'Grand Bugging' amendment.[103] The surveillance theorist Dörte Zbikowski describes this change to Article 13 of the U.S. Constitution in the following way:

In 1998 the article was changed to such an extent that technical devices may now be used to obtain evidence by means of acoustic surveillance of accommodation, but also of lawyer's offices, and doctor's surgeries, chartered accounts, spiritual advisors, in fact all those who, on the grounds of their profession, *are entitled to refuse evidence...* (my emphasis).[104]

If one needs a popular example of how offensive this kind of state sanctioned eves-dropping is to the ideals of democratic individualism, one need only be reminded of a seemingly unobjectionable plot point from Christopher Nolan's The Dark Knight. In what is perhaps the most absurd turn of events in the entire film, Bruce Wayne's top-secret technical assistant, Lucius Fox (played by Morgan Freedman), refuses to turn the whole of Gotham into a giant (pan)Acousticon in order to pin-point the location of the Joker and save a great number of Gotham's citizenry. Even though Lucius is regularly conscripted to attain and invent every kind of illegal ordinance for Batman's adventures; *and* he also organizes and coordinates Batman's ability to drop in and out of foreign countries against all judico-legal agreements about extradition and the like; *and* he also disregards every decree of lawful conduct in assisting the caped crusader in carrying out various forms of vigilante style justice — Lucius is nonetheless hit by the call of conscience when confronted with the request to violate the sanctity of cell phone communication. He only agrees to carry out Batman's plan on the condition that his resignation is confirmed in the aftermath of the current crisis — apparently as a matter of personal integrity and honor for a code of conduct that seems incredibly arbitrary unless one accounts for the audience to whom it is addressed.

This sort of absurdity is only plausible as a ruse that makes the film more appealing to its intended audience because acoustic surveillance is still the site of an original trauma in western consciousness — and even the obscene core of Panoptic power today. This is true not only because it defies the judico-legal protections accorded 'private' citizens and especially the intimacy associated with phone conversations, but also because revisionary Panopticism has already overdetermined the field of surveillance to such a degree as to make acoustic observation redundant. This is the real unmentionable of unmentionables in the situation — that the techniques of audio-visual surveillance redouble the power of observation in such a way that the suspension of democratic rights is confirmed without contestation. Ultimately, this is also why Lucius must resign, his actions represent the horror of the rights of the innocent turned against themselves for their own protection — and it is this perversion of justice alone that he cannot abide.[105]

4.16 The Acousticon as the Fourth Variation on Intensive and Extensive Social Control: The Primacy of Audio-Visual Techniques in the Organization of Knowledge/Power as a Subjectivizing Apparatus.

As offensive as this conflicted state of affairs is, we should still ask, is there another, even more pressing reason why the Acousticon must be passed over in every discussion of contemporary forms of Power/Knowledge outside of being the site of a repressed truth. Is it just the idea that hyper-Panoptic control forecloses the political prospects of anonymity, and that (pan)Acousticism enacts the real end of 'private' life as-such, or is there some other issue driving this forced sense of repression?

While everything mentioned above is certainly upsetting enough in its own right, the real point of significance that informs these issues is offered up by a second film of note, the HBO documentary, Terror in Mumbai. Released about a year after The Dark Knight, this shot by shot account of one of the worst terrorist incidents in India's history reveals that the very first strategy mentioned by the police in trying to locate the perpetrators, the origin of the operation and its current objectives, was none other than the need to scan the totality of the available audio spectrum. What is shown here, quite unabashedly, is that (pan)Acousticism occupies *a primary position* in the diagram of control today — especially in relation to the 'state of exception' (neo-sovereign rule). It is the power most often invoked by first responders as well as the absent center of Panoptic control, i.e., the place of a double repression based on judico-legal permissions. As such, the triangulation of audio-surveillance currently makes 'pan'-optic power a rejoinder to policing operations where auditory surveillance is regularly followed by visual scanning. This realization, or re-orientation toward the visual field, makes the Foucaultian genealogy of western power feel somewhat shortsighted for not acknowledging how Acousticism drives and divides Panoptic measures.

And while there is no need to assume this will continue to be the case in a future filled with newer technologies, increasing miniaturization and new categories of data-veillance, the primacy attributed to (pan)Acousticism is an accurate description of today's surveillance protocols. At the opening of the new century *the Acousticon represents the fourth figure of pre-modern power come back to haunt the (post-)modern age — and it is also the fourth instance of an intensive and extensive increase in Panopticism posited under the sign of sovereign practices of governmentality vis-à-vis the deployment of audio-visual techniques.*

However, the key insight provided by the Acousticon is not just its place of primacy in the hierarchy of surveillance, nor its proto-Panoptic impetus, but rather, that it represents a kind of power that cannot, or has not yet, been naturalized by the body socius. By and large, this omission persists because its explicit inclusion in the fourfold diagram of observational power provides both a concrete context for understanding Power/Knowledge in the audio-visual field as well as the possibility of naming the types of power relations that are operative in neo-Panoptic regimes, i.e., their interlocking configurations, their geographic permutations, their judicio-legal variations, their cartographic impositions, etc., etc. In other words, the Acousticon is what makes the diagram of power quantifiable and analyzable in societies of control — *it is the alpha and omega figure of contemporary relations of Power/Knowledge.*

More importantly however, is how the fusion of Panopticism and Acousticism represents an unspeakable violence that opens onto the erasure of democratic life by making the 'state of exception' a technique of governance rather that a declarative injunction like marshal law or enforced curfews. In fact, Pan-Acousticism is not only related to the supersession of lawful conduct in extreme circumstances, but it also demarcates the reconfiguration of lawful conduct tout court. With the rise of Pan-Acousticism, sovereign rule returns as a form of democratic imperialism that thoroughly integrates the structures of surveillance and subjectivation that have dominated the last few centuries of western life — only now they have the benefit of technological efficacy. And yet, this new assemblage of subjectivizing powers still begs the question, how do we understand the type of power that issues from the field of Pan-Acoustic control? How do we define the terms of social accommodation and refutation that are engendered by electronic Pan-Acousticism? And finally, how has the Pan-Acousticon become a biopolitical force that threatens to go beyond the regime of optic control — and even beyond debates about discipline and affective interpellation? These pressing questions will be the focus of our final two meditations on the architecture of power.

FIFTH MEDITATION

Social Control Between Panopticism and Fiberopticism

The passage to a society of control does not in any way mean the end of discipline — that is, the self-disciplining of subjects, the incessant whisperings of disciplinary logics within subjectivities themselves — is extended even more generally in the society of control. What has changed is that, along with the collapse of the institutions, the disciplinary dispositifs have become less limited and bounded spatially in the social field. Carceral discipline, school discipline, factory discipline, and so forth weave in a hybrid production of subjectivity. In effect, in the passage to the society of control, the elements of transcendence of disciplinary society decline while the immanent spaces are accentuated and generalized.

The immanent production of subjectivity in the society of control corresponds to the axiomatic logic of capital, and their resemblance indicates a new and more complete compatibility between sovereignty and capital.[106]

Michael Hardt & Antonio Negri

It may be predicted that 'taking care' of our virtual double(s) will develop into a major preoccupation, de-centering the earlier focus on the Self and its image in the eyes of others. The proposed concept of the surveillance-directed type may be helpful in tracing and exploring these processes. If true, these changes would render obsolete the earlier socio-psychological theories on the interiorization of social control as well as Foucault's ideas on technologies of the self. Indeed, the whole notion of working on our real selves to achieve ethically/socially desirable results is becoming pointless as our care is refocused on a virtual sphere populated by our potential clones.

The data-double becomes a key reference, which allows individuals to assess themselves in a relevant context while by-passing the Self of the socialized 'me'... once this hollowed-out self becomes virtually a mirror for surveillance, *the social* is consumed by whatever system rationally shapes and fuels that surveillance.[107]

Maria Los

We note the de-multiplicative power of the Benthamic device: for a maximum number of watched, it requires a minimum number of watchers; an apparent plethora conceals a parsimonious reality. But its powers actually create an all-seeing omnipresent, omniscient body that condemns the inhabitants to a dependency that no ordinary person can emulate, a body that is very like some fabricated God.

The Panopticon is a machine that creates a semblance of God. Is this not what Bentham must have had in mind when he used the following verses of the 139th Psalm as the heading for one of the numerous "perceptions" he addressed to the powers that be concerning his plan?

Thou art about my path, and about my bed: and spiest out my ways.

If I say, peradventure the darkness shall cover me, then shall my night be turned into day.

Even there also shall thy hand lead me; and thy right hand shall hold me.[108]

Jacques-Alain Miller

5.1 Rethinking the Design(s) of Neo-Panoptic Power in the Twenty-First Century: Bio-Power Between Totalizing Apparatuses and Totalitarian Assemblages.

Before elucidating the various models of critical and popular resistance to architectural power there is still one more pressing question that needs to be addressed — namely, what kind of power is constituted by revisionary Panopticism? Certainly, the fourfold diagram of neo-Panoptic control aims to be a totalizing power, but is it a totalitarian power — or even a form of soft totalitarianism?

While totalitarianism certainly affords us a starting point to investigate architectural interpolation as a 'totalizing' effect, this is only possible if we first address the conceptual determinations associated with totalitarianism as a social and political phenomena. The Merriam-Webster dictionary provides a concise definition of totalitarianism as split between the exercise of: "1) centralized control by an autocratic authority, and 2) the political concept that the citizen should be totally subject to an absolute state authority".[109] This discrete explanation of totalitarianism provides us with a Hegelian example of why this form of governance can never be a stopping point on the way to political freedom, i.e., because it is the image of a relation between the state and the individual that amounts to being something of a non-relation.

While this cursory definition provides us with a starting point for understanding how totalitarianism is framed in layman's terms, or even in simple philosophical terms, it is still necessary to engage in a more thoroughgoing examination of totalitarianism and its presuppositions beyond these pragmatic qualifiers. In this regard, the work of Maria Los provides us with a much broader description of the totalitarian drive as it has come to be associated with forms of surveillance and Panoptic control. For her, totalitarian power is (1) a global project that "knows no rational limit"; (2) it is the "belief in a hidden power... where the meaning of every law is secret"; (3) it is a power that is "arbitrary, (and) predicated on fear" and which demands "infinite malleability and obedience"; and (4) it is a power that dominates its subjects through "social atomization, de-tradition-alization... and the radial destruction of trust".[110] Above all else, Los considers totalitarianism to be (5) a deeply de-socializing power built upon a "taboo mentality" that permits no deviation from the norm — a great hollowing out of the truth of the self, morality and action in inter-subjective relations.[111]

Starting with this as our operative definition of totalitarian rule, can hyper Panopticism be thought of as instituting these kinds of social, or really, anti-social relations? Does the fourfold diagram of power match the five conditions provided by Los, or does it fall short of being a functional parallel to totalitarianism — and if this is the case, then what kind of power is produced by contemporary Panopticism? And is it even a power for which we have a proper name?

5.2 Neo-Panoptic Power as an Assemblage of Subjectivizing Effects: Interrogatory, Enterrogatory and Inferrogatory Forms of Interpellation.

However conflicted our investigations into the nature of Panoptic power might seem, however unorthodox our determi-nations might read, and however mixed and illegible our conclusions might prove to be, let us at least attempt to provide an answer to each and every one of Los's five traits. While this is no easy task within the confines of language, which often fails to capture the lived experience of neo-Panopticism in its subtle and nuanced forms; its networked systems of capture and subjection; and its dynamic and complex processes of subjectivation — such is the task set forth here as a matter to be pursued point by point.

First Point: Totalitarianism is a global project without rational limit.

The fourfold diagram of power is not only without rational limit but it is without a natural limit in regard to its technological applications. As such, we might be able to say that techno-Panopticism is even without an *irrational limit* — or that its rational expansion proceeds irrationally and is only structurally coordinated and integrated into the social functioning of power after the fact. In this regard, revisionary Panopticism cannot be characterized as a totalitarian power in the sense of being centrally orchestrated and globally planned. It is more of a defacto power, or a kind of ad-hoc totalitarianism — or even just an assemblage power that attempts to be totalizing without ever achieving such an end because it consists of mixed cartographies of subjective control. In opposition to totalitarian governance, neo-Panopticism is focused on the (in)dividual as an object of appropriation, or even as an object of self-appropriation. While both share the abstract dream of expansive control, totalitarianism seeks to institute a state of grand uniformity among its subjects while neo-Panopticism manufactures subjective deformity. Or, to put it somewhat differently, totalitarianism is turned against the 'outside' world while revisionary Panopticism is turned against the world of interiority. This however, does not make (neo)Panoptic control a totalitarian regime — at least, not in any way that is historically recognizable.

Second Point: Totalitarianism is the belief in a hidden power where the meaning behind every law is secret.

The fourfold diagram of power requires both the belief that it exists for its effectivity and the maintenance of its disavowal for its affectivity. As such, it is a twofold force of interpolation, being both an exponential power of record and a subjectivizing process composed of interrogatory, enterrogatory and inferrogatory relations. In short, revisionary Panopticism is a highly mitigated power which presupposes that nothing is hidden and that everything can *and should be* known. In fact, its true totalitarian potential lies in an incontestable drive toward externalization and total transparency, i.e., in its ability to be 'all-seeing' while continuously constructing intra- and supra-observational forms of capture where everything is given to be seen, (even that which properly escapes corporeal vision). In such a scenario, being and being-seen become synonymous — existence is confirmed by passing through an endless series of ciphers that actively dissect and catalog the visible world.

Consequently, revisionary Panopticism is not really totalitarian in nature however 'totalizing' it may be. We could even say that hyper Panopticism is hegemonic without creating what Gramsci would have called a hegemonic block — or that it dominates its subjects without deploying centrifugal forms of power.[112] While the forcible directedness of totalitarian rule represents a power based on straight lines — lines of command, lines of flight, and gestural lines of the body held taunt in both greeting and salute — the regime of hyper-Panopticism is a spiraling power: everywhere elongated, supple and curvilinear, (the superstructural organization and (re)production of bloated baroque bodies, enflamed organs, and engorged physiques). Unlike the selective focus of the totalitarian gaze hyper Panoptic control is constructed by a coiling power or an encircling function. Its serpentine design is composed of absentee operators that operate nonetheless — and even when neo-Panopticism actually has operators they usually operate on nothing in particular — or just on the coordination of nothing but particulars. Neo-Panopticism relies more on sorting and cross-referencing data streams rather than actually watching and/or concealing specific acts, activities or actors. Technopticism is by and large a regulatory power rather than an enforced power — a

'Pan'-optic power of the sovereign seven-headed hydra rather than the statist symbols of the eagle, the lion or the bull.

The only 'secret' of revisionary Panopticism is its power of revealing — and this secret is actually the subversion of 'the secretive' tout court. Neo-Panopticism even proposes the end of all plausible conspiracy theories through totalized watching. Or, we could say that within the fourfold diagram of neo-Panoptic power, the secret is finally displaced by the enigma, where nothing is withheld but everything waits in a state of floating suspension to be contextualized and correlated. If anything, revisionary Panopticism is closest to being a type of open-ended inclusivity that is characterized by the doublebind of generating statistics and status reports without goal or motivation. Once again, this appears to be a kind of inverted totalitarianism at best.

Third Point: Totalitarianism is an arbitrary power predicated on fear that demands infinite malleability and obedience from its subjects.

The fourfold diagram of power today is neither arbitrary nor necessarily predicated on fear. It is immanent, omnipresent, and strategic, but it is not random — it is really anything but random. In contrast to totalitarianism, neo-Panopticism actively shapes itself to the malleability of its subjects rather than the other way around. Certainly, the motivational impetus behind neo-Panopticism relies on the hope of future remuneration and the threat of future criminalization, but this only happens at the level of unconscious and preconscious motivation(s). Hyperbolic Panopticism is largely considered to be *pre-corrective* — an operative form of silent social interventionism or supra-subjec-tivizing incentivism.

Consequently, the diagram of power associated with hyper Panopticism is not really totalitarian inasmuch as it favors self-modulation over adjudicated obedience and weak stratified power over strong corrective demands. Following this third set of contrasting qualifiers, we can say that neo-Panopticism is closer to being something like a form of consumerist totalitarianism or totalized consumerist subjectivation — where any evidence of the totalitarian drive is only present in a minor key.

Fourth Point: Totalitarianism dominates its subjects through social atomization, de-traditionalization and the radical destructuration of trust.

The fourfold diagram of power does not dominate its subjects through 'social atomization' and 'de-traditionalization' so much as it displaces tradition through dividuation. Or, much more radically, it makes dividuation into tradition, and most especially, into the set of daily rituals that fortify subjective insularity. In post-industrial societies the subject is saturated through and through by information and insecurity — and as Los has noted, "in becoming digitized, the individual ceases to be the basic and indivisible unit of society and society itself becomes converted into a series of non-social identities such as numerical samples, databases and virtual markets".[113] Paradoxically, in this new situation, dividuals come to trust in the fourfold diagram of power that much more, usually as a means of eluding any encounter with radical forms of otherness. However, what is much harder to perceive, is that this same diagram of control also makes it possible to avoid encountering any sense of sameness posited as indexical consumerist identicality. If anything, revisionary Panopticism tends to follow the logic of the excluded middle, or rather, it produces and reproduces the modulated middling dividual, (non-contestual consciousness).

Yet, to be considered totalitarian, societies of surveillance would need both a strong power of subjective command and strong subjects to internalize it. Currently, *it has neither*. De-traditionalization and social (sub)atomization have more to do with the unlimited expansion of worker time and the subsumption of (in)dividuals into the three great commercial-communes of our day: planned communities, virtual communities and sub-cultural communities — as well as every other form of post-familial/post-cultural 'togetherness'. In the final analysis, the destructuration of trust is now exercised more effectively by dividuals against themselves rather than an/other, and particularly in over-identifying with being taken as a 'thing' of observation.[114] In many ways, this is simply the negative image of totalitarian control — or of totalizing negativity toward desubjectivation and/or resubjectivation beyond the regime of hyper-capitalist/neo-Panoptic control.

Fifth Point: Totalitarianism is a deeply de-socializing power built upon a taboo mentality that permits no deviation from the norm.

The fourfold diagram of power is not so much de-socializing as it is hyper-socializing, capturing its subjects in a recursive loop of unending observation and virtual interactivity dispersed across spaces of corporeal isolation and dividuated penitentarism. Neo-Panopticism destroys the power of the taboo by replacing it with a strictly paranoiac function, where all illicit activities are encouraged but only at the expense of showing up on ones digital dossier at some later date. If anything, the supposed 'hollowing out' of the totalitarian subject is here displaced by a hyper-sensitized 'filling up' that is associated with the saturated subject of anxiety, self-immolation and pathological neurosis. In other words, it is a subject that only 'hollows itself out' through unintended incrimination, pharmaceutical suffocation and intensive self-suspicion. As such, the dividuated subject suffers from an entirely different configuration of social oppression than what totalitarianism provides for — in any or all of its means.

The neo-Panoptic environment is a space where the destructuration of trust *isn't* exercised by intimidation and refutation but by circulation and provocation, i.e., by the fact that deeply trusting relationships are never given the means, time or anonymous social space to thrive and develop. In control societies social-being mirrors the soft and immaterial forms of production that permeate a radically de-socialized/hyper-socialized world of exchange — where 'interactivity' and 'inter-subjective relations' largely consist of the multiplication of light interactions, tertiary acquaintanships, and virtual transactions. Even sexual relations have been commuted into booty calls, FwB's (Friends with benefits), simulated pleasures and every other possible form of denatured touching.

As such, neo-Panopticism is not a power built on adherence to 'the norm' but really a totalitarianism of self-initiated subjection — a radically internalized power of sub-atomizing self-inqui-sition that naturalizes the weightlessness of transitive associa-tions and social mutability. In counter-distinction to the work of the philosopher-psychoanalyst Felix Guattari, we could say that control societies and neo-capitalism tend to induce *molecular involutions* rather than *molecular revolutions.* Or, following on the observations of Gilles Deleuze we could say that control societies bring about the restructuration of intensities, feelings, and every sort of becoming — ultimately producing a highly stratified anti-revolutionary society, or really, a sub-atomized pacification society. Even Lyotard's characterization of the capitalist apparatus as a libidinal force of sorts falls short of describing the predicament of dividuated subjects circumscribed by integrated exchange and social ionization.[115] Certainly, Lyotard's character-ization of the erotics of production and the perverse enjoyment of debauched subjection still ring true, but none of these descrip-tions of the de-socialized body of hyperbolic capital issue from a totalitarian tenor — or as Lyotard would say, a totalitarian *tensor.*[116]

In conclusion, we cannot really say that revisionary

Panopticism is more of a totalitarian power than its eighteenth or nineteenth century counterparts, or even that Panopticism was ever defined by the totalitarian urge to begin with. If anything, it is a *post-totalitarian* form of power. But if this is indeed the case, then how can we describe the event of Panoptic appropriation in positive terms, i.e., around what designations are we to define the contemporary diagram of control as a totalizing force that is also an eccentric power?

5.3 Neo-Panopticism, the Post-historical Condition and the Persistence of Disparate Models of Subjectivation: The Integration of Sovereign-Metaphysical, Disciplinary-Rational and Capitalist-Immanentist Apparatuses of Control.

Certainly, neo-Panopticism is not a form of soft totalitarianism, fascism, or even a micro-physics of self-regulating power — although all of these forms of organizing the body socius do inform how we think about the exercise of power in control societies today, especially as a recombant or hybrid force. Even so, neo-Panopticism still requires a complete revision of how we conceptualize inter-subjective relations, psychic subjection and socio-economic subjectivation.

Unlike totalitarianism, the hyper Panoptic regime represents a much more formal power, or rather, it is posited as being such. One could even say that contemporary forms of Panoptic control appear that much more perverse for having finally made the absent center of religious obedience and the strong center of rationalist instruction co-extensive — in essence, (mis)taking both of these forms of subjective interpellation for formal operations.

Perhaps this is what the move from macro to micro to sub-atomizing power is — a co-constitutive (re)configuration of power 'types', (Synoptic, Banoptic, Bio-optic and Acoustic), placed under the sign of formulaic efficiency, systemic determinations and axiomatic functions. This transitive property of power relations could even be characterized as a distinctive admixture of (pre-modern) belief, (modern) instrumental reason and (postmodern) technocratic rule, where the last of these three dispositif's incorporates and updates each prior regime of control through an exhaustive moment of Panoptic synthesis — or even a synthetic recombination of disciplinary dispositif's.

But here a short digression is in order because the trap of believing in 'progress' — or in progressive models of control — is that the simplifications attributable to periodization often erase the persistence of prior models of subjectivation. In so doing, the heterogeneity of 'historical' life is reduced to reified generalizations that make it impossible to understand how pre-modern forms of subjectivation manage to subsist beneath new forms of social control. In drawing out a cartography of contemporary power this is a grave error because 'progress' moves not so much by transformations as mutations; not so much by inventing new universes as multiplying retroverses; not so much by clear divisions of innovation as accounting for metastasized apparatuses of cultural condensation. From Hegel to Fukuyama the idea of 'progress' is often used as a misnomer of sorts for compounding and redoubling efforts here, diversifying and mystifying applications there, and refining and complexifying the play of reversibility everywhere. Or, to quote Baudrillard on the paradoxes of historical interlocution in the (post)postmodern era: "History has only wrenched itself from cyclical time to fall into the order of the recyclable."[117] Of course, the problem here is in picturing just what this means, i.e., of understanding what forms, for one reason or another, were neither "degradable" nor "disposable" — especially with regard to different regimes of social control.[118] We must finally confront why it is that *History will not come to an end*, which is the same as saying we must try to understand why History will not begin again as a 'true' history, as a 'real' history or as a history after history.[119]

In no uncertain terms, this is the paradoxical position

attributed to post-historical existence — of having to endure the untimeliness of time itself; of passing through a time *out of time;* of experiencing the brute repetitions of uncontrollable iterability, matriculation and even a semi-farcical state of speaking about 'historical' affairs. In other words, this is the burden of a distinctly postmodern sense of time which opens onto the conundrum of infinite replayability and hyperbolic co-option. To Marx's original formulation, "History happens twice, first as tragedy, then as farce" we could now add, that History happens only once, and then always over and ever again[120] — as a variation of the Benjaminian Now-Time of the present.[121]

In the case of Panopticism however, this de-sequencing simply means that mystical, sovereign and disciplinary apparatuses of control continue to persist alongside subjectivizing designs, even emptied of the strong beliefs which gave rise to their deployment in another milieu. It should be no surprise that every new generation seeks to make use of a series of contingent potentials from the dispositif's of another age. In fact, this is what neo-Panopticism teaches us today — that power is endlessly (re)appropriated and always searches out a new means of deployment — even among the most outmoded and subterranean of propositions.

This integral approach shows itself wherever the formal dimension of power associated with Enlightenment practices of discipline (Panopticism), and the absolutist dream of the inquisition (Panacousticism), are co-mingled through the unlimited extension of technological means (techno-Panacousticism). This new frame of observation everywhere proclaims its freedom from ideological bias, but such is the error of our times — *even the defining illusion of the day.* Freed of suspicion, the 'all-seeing' machine (Panopticism) and 'all-hearing' devices (Panacousticism) finally take on their properly metaphysical dimension through the double articulation of audio-visual techniques. Together, they represent a super-added dimension of control associated with

Panoptic mechanisms that is far beyond the reach of nineteenth and twentieth century technologies.

5.4 Monadism, Hyper-Capitalism and Indo-Colonization: Rethinking Leibniz and the Calculus of Social Physics.

As such, the fourfold diagram of power is everywhere expanding its affective domain through the deployment of two socio-psychological vectors: omniscient simulation and omnipresent virtuality. If we were to name it, revisionary Panopticism is closest to being a metaphysical power in the sense of constituting not only an 'all-hearing' and 'all-seeing' assemblage, but also in producing an 'all-knowing' judico-legal apparatus. Yet this term is something of a misnomer because metaphysics is too strongly associated with the beyond, the transcendental and the super-sensible. In counter-distinction to the commonplace conception of otherworldly belief, hyper-Panopticism has enacted the greatest reconfiguration of subjective experience since the birth of Christianity — even sanctifying the spread of de-worlding belief (economic de-regulation, infrastructural de-cay, environmental de-gradation, social de-sertion, subjectivizing de-ification, resource de-pletion, etc., etc.). We might even say that neo-Panopticism is an oblique qualifier for the production of what Alain Badiou calls an atonal world (monde atone) — or the production of a world that lacks "the intervention of a Master-signifier to impose meaningful order onto the confused multiplicity of reality."[122] Perhaps this is even the best way to understand the rise of neo-Panopticism and control societies — as the production of four distinctive disciplinary dispositif's that try to compensate for an irreducible lack. Or, to go one step further, we could even say that *neo-Panopticism is the Master-signifier of the postmodern era,* qualified as it is, by sovereign practices of governmentality, disciplinary experts and security specialists.

Additionally, the type of power associated with the present

regime of Panopticism — or even the production of presence particular to the 'Pan'-optic — could be characterized as a neo-colonial or self-colonizing power that seeks to destroy the world of interiority by externalizing it. This is because neo-Panopticism exteriorizes intimacy, subjective inflections, private intimations and can even be posited as unworking the seat of the soul if the soul is taken as that particular fold of subjective reflection that conceives of its actions as being of everlasting consequence, (or even of practical consequence). But how is this achieved — how is the Judeo-Christian notion of the soul itself restricted, destructured and unfolded? Or finally, how is the same process a function of naturalizing criminality in democratic life?

The most straightforward, albeit provisional answer, to such a question, is that neo-Panopticism creates a new fold in the process of subjectivation that makes the metaphysical dimension of sovereign judgment immanent to this life — and even to the experience of daily life. Revisionary Panopticism institutes a regime of endless self-inspection that is provided for by subjects who are partially or wholly unaware of becoming permanent objects of judicial, legal and technological inspection. Hyperbolic Panopticism is not just a power of concrete transparency, but a play of possible subject positions that relies on the assumption of an operative, but invisible dimension of surveillance that circumscribes the totality of everyday acts, actions, interactions and transactions. It is a regime of control that is invested by capital and law to the same degree that it is divested of an otherworldly dimension, (or even of the common historical horizon of political, scientific, artistic or inter-subjective 'worlds'). In this regard, hyperbolic capital sanctions and makes possible a form of control that is everywhere within reach — *a radical metaphysics immanent to the field of circumspect sociality.*

Ironically, neo-capitalism has even been defended as a form of protection against the proposition(s) of metaphysical reduction at the very same moment that it threatens to become a force that is more-than-metaphysical, i.e., an instrumental metaphysics raised to the power of absolute efficiency. This new metaphysic, (based on suspicion rather than superstition), is even something like a virtual power: more simulated than present, more operative than functional, and even more imagined than real — however much its concrete manifestations still overdetermine the field of sociability through the multiplication of interpolative effects. Consequently, the (in)dividuated subject is not just a weak subject caught up in the networked forces of revisionary Panopticism, or even what Foucault called the 'mircro-physics' of (social) power. Instead, the process of subjectivation is now co-constitutive with a sub-atomizing power that colonizes the modern monad in total.

As a result, we find ourselves returned to the seventeenth century picture of subjectivity not only because the monad is the perfected image of the telematic (in)dividual, but because Leibniz formulated a theory of subjectivity whereby, once a monad is breached, or internalizes a colonial force in even the smallest measure, it is then quickly colonized in its entirety. While Leibniz used this metaphor to mean something like the power of human contiguity, i.e., the taking hold of the mind by a certain processual constigular relation of thoughts, ideas and beliefs — today (indo)colonization has become synonymous with the active production of self-sanctification, class-(de)strati-fication and admittance to the identifactory-industrial-complex. Everywhere hyper-capital transforms the monad, taken as a world *unto it-self*, into a world *about it-self* – not so much a Monadology of subjective effects but a homology of subjec-tivizing distortions based on hyper-atomization.

Among Leibniz's many notable contributions he also provided us with something like the first theory of memes, (and perhaps even addiction), by underscoring the relation of casually over-determined connections. All that was required to secure a concrete analysis of subjectivation in our social milieu was to posit these operations alongside Leibniz's diagram of the soul, i.e., the house with two floors.[123] How else do we think about the process of indo-colonization at the opening of the twenty-first century other than as (home) invasion, the reification of consciousness (self-petrification), the appropriation of emotional states (self-obfuscation), and the addictive hold of the self (self-deification/neo-narcissism)? These are the four conditions that put us after alienation, estrangement, ideology and false consciousness. Instead, we have come to speak of the expropriation of consciousness as nothing less than a force of systemic, pharmalogical, socio-economic collusion — or of a growing indentifactory-industrial-complex without measure, limits or judico-legal constraints.

5.5 Beyond Neo-Panoptic Control: Fiberopticism and the Power to Affect the Fibrous Dimension of Being Through Electro-Synaptic Automations.

If anything, revisionary Panopticism relies on a different activation of the affections than Panopticism proper. It is a power of hyper-consciousness, hyper-visibility and hyper-activity grounded in techniques of pre-criminalization, personalization and retroversive predestination. In simple terms, it is a power of emulation (Synopticism), judicio-legal rule (Banopticism), biological invasiveness (Bio-opticism) and sovereignty (Pan-Acousticism), but this in no way accounts for its emergent effects. The fourfold diagram of neo-Panopticism is a force of perceptual interpolation that pre-exists the social field; it even calls it forth; constructs its various spaces and subjects; modulates their inter-actions, feelings and ambitions; catalogs their movements and associations; captures their faces and expressions; produces their data-doubles and their virtual doppelgangers, etc. It is an endemic, immersive, extensive process of subjectivation that takes autonomy, anonymity and the autocratic self to be relics of the modern world-view that must still undergo further destructuration — *far beyond what we are already experiencing today.* The accelerated and still accelerating pace of (re)production may even include the obliteration of the democratic body *by necessity* — or at least, the total suppression of every principle of democratic participation that disrupts the demands of big Capital.

If the fourfold diagram of control could be given a singular name; one that exceeds its seventeenth and eighteenth century designs by realizing them; one which pertains to the rule of technocratic logic and bureaucratic justification; one which captures something of its intensive and extensive dimensions; one which points to the supersession of all previous paradigms of control including the radical potential to transcend and overcome its own limitations — such a name would have to be found in the dubious title of Fiberopticism, (a term that our generation has already naturalized and mythologized). Fiberopticism has been enshrined in the glowing circuitry of blockbuster films like the Matrix, Tron and Avatar to name only a few. Almost from its inception, the Fiberoptic apparatus called forth an intangible life-force, a new nervous system of electro-connectivity and a new metaphysic based on internal illumination rather than an otherworldly glow. But in what does this new dimension of control consist — and how is it made to function with any consistency? How is it internalized, externalized and realized throughout the fabric of social being? And is Fiberopticism the final overturning of neo-Panopticism or just the newest dimension of Panoptic subjectivation?

As an articulated force of control Fiberopticism is something like the unlimited power to effect the fibrous dimension of being through electro-affective intimations, i.e., projections (Synopticism), prohibitions (Banopticism), subjection (Bio-opticism) and subjectivation (Pan-Acousticism). It is the sign of our fading belief in a higher power as well as the demand for a heightened power of subjective control — *a virile and viral replacement metaphysics to compensate for the death of God.* It is even a limit event in our understanding of the techniques of social control — one which reaches inside the electro-synaptic automations of being to retrieve, reconfigure and recall every last trace of error or prohibited action.

We could even go so far as to say that the first sign of Fiberopticism emerged in 1938 with the invention of electroshock therapy, (now called electroconvulsive therapy). However, yesterday's psychoanalytic cure is often today's new disciplinary technique! Now taser guns are just another legalized form of hijacking bodily functions from the inside out, (or the naturalization of electro-convulsive discipline). The second moment of Fiberoptic subjectivation is synonymous what the French philosopher Paul Virilio calls 'cultural cathodization' — or the development of early models of electro-entertainment that subjected spectators to a continual flow of electrons that issued from the hot filaments of pre-digital technologies. For Virilio, the birth of modern teleoscopy was really the dawn of inorganic consciousness and Fiberoptic (indo)colonization, or what Debord called the process of spectacularization. And yet, in our contemporary moment, Virilio sees the spread of 'cathodic globalization' as sanctifying the "new orthodoxy of the 'single brain'... disguised behind (the) persistent notion of REVOLUTION: meaning, a telecommunications revolution that 'research promoters' never stop boasting is inevitable."[124] But beneath these rather poignant polemics the Fiberoptic regime is becoming much more pervasive and interconnected than anything Virilio ever proposed.

Over the course of the last few decades, Fiberopticism has been concretized by the deployment of nano-technologies (the invasive discipline and monitoring of the body), the procurement and extraction of visual memories (electroptic discipline), the development of gene therapy (di-agnostic-discipline), and the growing acceptance of the organ trade (evisceration discipline).[125] Here we have another repetition of pre-modern,

modern and postmodern models of social control that are wholly emergent — and even an entirely new fourfold apparatus that exceeds the designs of revisionary Panopticism.[126] Yet the most downplayed threat of Fiberopticism is still the rise of data conscious and radical advancements in the carrying capacity of associative neural nets — a change that may bring about the singularity of post-human consciousness. Without a doubt, these developments in A.I. are quickly approaching the possibility of reproducing inhuman watchers that are something more-than-human, where cyberoptic Panopticism becomes the central dispositif of subjectivation and/or archio-(disciplinary)-attunement.

5.6 Absolutist Subjectivation: The Fiberoptic (re)Ordering of Being, (or Being Without Discipline).

But is Fiberopticism anything other than the will-toward increasing technicity — and does it qualitatively supersede (neo)Panopticism? Is Fiberopticism a supra-added affect, a supernova effect, or just another fold in interpolative power? Is the fiber-'optic' a diagram which unfolds the designs of revisionary Panopticism, or is it a force which refolds its subjectivizing dimensions into an entirely different model of subjectivation?

Undoubtedly, Fiberopticism is situated at the nexus point of these concerns and contradictions — being a regime that is both the summation of neo-Panoptic designs and also the moment of its radical overturning. Certainly, this mutation in subjectivizing apparatuses is co-constitutive with the rise of control societies, where the legalization of internalized observation, indo-colonization and electro-discipline means that the electro-eye (cameras) is sure to be superseded by the extraction of sentient perception (sense-data). Everywhere this latest dimension of archio-discipline — of fiber-optics entering fibrous being — is focused on reconstructing brain waves to represent visual images, re-sequencing DNA to resemble 'natural' and sometimes very unnatural forms of life, and reconfiguring every possible form of enterrogatory subjectivation. Without any sense of reserve, it is finally Fiberopticism that has come to represent the instrumentalization of perception in all of its material determinations — it is even the movement from properly interrogatory regimes of control to enterrogatory apparatuses of investment, i.e., of indo-colonization as the reordering of species-being.

This new fold in Panopticism may finally be the subjective knot which represents the end of any real need for global Penitentiarism, (even though it will surely persist as a means of audio-visual confirmation and subjective conformation/deformation). If these radical forms of subjectivizing power continue to find new applications as an internal diagram of extraction, we may soon return to an analysis of totalitarian power, or hyper-totalitarianism, or even electro-totalitarianism — realizing that neo-Panopticism was only ever a transitional phase on the way to a truly foreboding horizon of surveillance. One day we might even speak of hyper-subjectivation without any need for 'correction' or 'training' at all. Fiberopticism can, and may very well be, the institution of a strictly tautological totalitarian power — an example of neo-Panopticism raised beyond its architectural premise(s) toward the absolutist territorialization of subjectivity, (or of determination in the first instance).

But certainly, this science fiction inspired form of social control only looms on the horizon as a real possibility — presenting us with a disquieting scenario where the final eye of observation will need to be sequestered not to tell its story, but to reveal its datum; where bodies will be disciplined by the digerati, or a new class of crypto-technical illuminati; where hyperbolic capitalism suddenly and irreversibly doubles over into fascist economics and labor eugenics; and where the zero sum game of capital becomes synonymous with the drive toward radical depopulation. The purest incarnation of Fiberopticism would be something like the production of confessors who need not be conversant; a legal system without the need for testimony; a body without need of subjective inspection; and a world of productive forces without goal — or the proliferation of auto-appropriative means without restriction — where the machinations of hyperbolic capital become truly autonomous from desire, design, intention, and necessity, (pure auto-valorization). Fiberopticism represents a form of cybernetic capitalism that we can only glimpse today — not so much *embodied capital* (affective capital) as *in-bodied capital* (total or radical subsumption).[127] This is the eventuality that even Horkheimer and Adorno could not have foreseen, that the racism implicit in western forms of rationality could be given voice through an entirely different critique of en-light-enment thinking (internal illumination).[128]

Running counter to the positivism of Donna Haraway's Cyborg Manifesto, the inheritance of the enlightenment draws to a close with the institution of electro-being rather than hybrid cyberism.[129] The Fiberoptic subject is not so much a post-human subject as it is an inhuman subject — a figure that is increasingly inorganic in all regards: the subject of the unlimited working day; of commodified relations of every imaginable kind; of hyperbolic surveillance that colonizes subjects through auto-reflexive means as well as corporatist memes; of broken down matter and an irradiated environment; of radical cultural co-dependency and emotional bi-polarity based on the heightened antagonisms internal to hyper-capital, not to mention the production and reproduction of post-communal, post-familial, and post-corporeal relations of every type and kind. As a historical motif, Fiberopticism is the figure of an estranged cyborg reality based on automaton consciousness — that other great fascination of the seventeenth century imagination. Yet today, it is the automation of the organic (automatism), rather than the organicism of the inorganic (cyborgism), that permeates the cultural unconscious.

Indeed, we may find in a very short time that the final eye of revisionary Panopticism is sure to be our own — and when these powers of architectural control are strictly internal, deployed against the body as a force of occupation rather than observation, even becoming an architectural appendage of the body itself, then, and only then, will (neo-)Panopticism be displaced by the rule of Fiberopticism. Then and only then, will we speak of a truly distended body — *the cogito in ruin* — rather than the productivities of a substantive body extended in space and community. Then and only then, will we look to A.I. for new forms of discipline, having forgotten the freedom of autonomous and de-instrumentalized living. Perhaps, such a folly could even lead to concretizing Fiberopticism as a system of metaphysics in line with the unholy trinity of today's futurists: hardware, software, and wetware in one — obedience to the Godhead of cyber-sentience and the archipelago of purely technical control, (the final 'pan'-optic-*con*).

In fact, we may even have to concede that this has already happened — or at the very least, that this kind of cultural transformation is already well underway. Everywhere around us, the belief that technology is closer too, or at least capable of capturing a trace of the super-sensible realm is becoming commonplace. If we have already given Fiberopticism an origin in psychoanalytic practice (electro-shock therapy), corporeal discipline (taser-guns) and technological development (the invention of the cathode), all that remains is to finally name its properly metaphysic dimension, i.e., its spectral figures. Such a task is perhaps best articulated through cinematic references, and the J-horror phenomena of the last few decades in particular, i.e., the many remakes of Japanese horror films about technological hauntings and electro-magnetic disturbances. However, movies like The Ring (2002, 2005, 2012), The Grudge (2004, 2006, 2009), White Noise (2005, 2007), and Pulse (2006, 2008) only provide an overview of the presuppositions of Fiberopticism when set against the backdrop of horror films from an earlier generation, like the techno-horror thriller Poltergeist (1982). While Poltergeist is often read as a tale of revenge that revolves around the spiritual (dis)possession of native American lands vis-à-vis urban sprawl, a more attentive reading of this subtext might focus on the divide between organic and inorganic consciousness, or the split between mystical and technological models of metaphysics.

Ever since little Carol Ann was pulled into another dimension through the television, there has been no end to the new forms of spectrography that claim to capture some trace of other-worldly beings — drawing a clear line between 'native', colonial and indo-colonial models of spiritual presencing. If mysticism revolves around incarnation and incantations, and sovereignty around the dictates of tradition and repetition, then the logos of techno-metaphysics is strictly determined by techniques of electro-capture. These might include, but are not limited to, the use of digital photography, night vision goggles, infrared filters, EMF meters (electro-magnetic detection), temperature measurements, digital and analog recording devices (EVP detection), Geiger counters, ion meters, ultrasonic motion sensors, air quality monitors, sound monitoring equipment, and so on and so forth. In short, the tools of techno-metaphysics are everywhere on display throughout the various ghost hunter programs that provide us with innumerable examples of how transubstantiation has been displaced by an interest in transfixation and its trace artifacts, i.e., nearly imperceptible variations in the electromagnetic field. But when did the shift toward Fiberopticism really begin, and how do we mark its entrance into the cultural imaginary as a dominant cinematic motif?

Of course, the dream of electro-being already attends the birth of the En-lighten-ment, especially if we take Mary Shelly's *Frankenstein* as a harbinger of things to come, (the figure of electro-being par excellence). Nevertheless, the ascension of

Technopticism in the popular mind follows from the naturalization of telematics throughout the late twentieth and early twenty-first centuries, reaching something of a tipping point in public awareness between the late 70s and the mid-80s. In much that same way that the Freddy Kruger films (1984, 1985, 1987, 1989, 1991, 1994, 2003, 2010, 2011) capitalized on bringing fear back to the suburbs; or The Toxic Avenger (1984) and The Swamp Thing (1982) embodied environmental concerns; or the return of Vampire films feed off the paranoia of the HIV epidemic; Carol Ann's abduction by demonic forces in Poltergeist came to stand-in for the greater abduction of a generation of children from inter-personal/familial relations — and in the J-horror context, from the state sanctioned abdication of children's rights.[130] Undoubtedly, the defining motif behind many of these techno-horror pictures is the predominance of latch-key kids and solitary children come back to haunt their neglectful and often, hateful parents. Both Carol Ann from Poltergeist and Samara from The Ring, (Sadako in original), only have a television for childhood companionship — or rather, they are the first captives of the televisual-cathodic apparatus. Or, to place this cultural problematic in strictly materialist terms, Carol Ann and Samara are the first casualties of 'the new socialization' where the effects of intensive subsumption are most easily discerned through (1) the absence of parental care and emotional attentiveness, (2) the demonstrative effects of rising inflation and the increasing need to have two working parents, and (3) the naturalization of work time in the home and the end of a properly delimited time of domesticity.[131]

But what is the big change that has occurred since Poltergeist made its debut — or between the figures of Carol Ann and Samara respectively? What is the surest sign of having become a Technoptic/Panoptic society other than the ubiquitous presence of technology? None other than the fact that films like The Ring, The Grudge, Pulse and White Noise portray deathly figures invading our world through so many different audio-visual apparatuses in an effort to get their life back, i.e., the time-of-life. They are, in short, allegories of metaphysical invasion about physical expropriation, in both this life and the next. But unlike Poltergeist and a great deal of Hollywood cinema, the J-horror films often end in abject failure, where the omnipresence of technology is not only seen as irreversible and unavoidable, but where it also serves as a model of radical contamination and indo-colonization. In fact, if Carol Ann marks the twilight of real subsumption and the fading relevance of a protected childhood, than Samara and the children of the J-horror films are the (dis)incarnated figures of radical subsumption come back to haunt the neglect of proper parental concern. In such films, the cathodic threat finally becomes immanent to this life, and the belief that technology is closer to the supernatural dimension than sentient perception begins to prevail. In these examples, as well as many other films, Technoptic control is pictured as The Final Destination (2000, 2003, 2006, 2009, 2011) of western culture — of death fated to be a figure of techne and nothing else — where capitalization and intensive subsumption reinforce the death drive as the socio-psychological dynamic that circum-scribes everyday existence.

But perhaps the most radical proclamation of the post-historical perspective on Technoptic positivism comes from movies far outside the horror genre, like the superhero block-buster movie Thor (2011), where Thor declares: "Your ancestor's called it magic, and you call it science, I come from a place where they're one and the same." From action films like Terminator (1984, 1991, 2003) to faked documentaries like Paranormal Activity (2007, 2010, 2011) to drama's like Frequency (2000), these new allegories make spectrality into a reality, where crossed signals and lost transmissions attempt to demonstrate how Fiberopticism is an über-metaphysic of sorts and even a new form of electro- or supra-naturalism. This is perhaps the great Fiberopti-*con* of our times — the final incarnation of instrumental rationalism — or of the cinematic dream of instrumental rationality raised beyond its formal presuppositions, (the standing-reserve of 'Man' as the subject of an incontrovertible electro-order).

There is, finally, a new specter haunting the cultural imaginary, and it is based on the threat of spectrality itself, i.e., of the reduction of organic life to a shadow of its former existence. Everywhere endemic anxiety, de-presenced corporeality, disembodied capital, immaterial production and the exhaustive circuit of precarious labor make life into a ghostly affair of perpetual possession by the subjectivizing apparatuses of affective capitalism and hyper Panoptic control. But above all else, what haunts the power of the bios today is the specter of Fiberopticism as an intangible blockage to the movement of the free spirit, i.e., the esprit of organic communion and the rejection of sovereign systems of judicio-legal rule. And yet, our best means of understanding this blockage of libratory potential is still that first system of controlled shadowy projects — the Panopticon. For as far as we are from Foucault's first observations on disciplinary mechanisms and biopower, his work has lost none of its force of urgency — save only a transmutation of its terms and conditions.

5.7 Sub-atomizing Subjectivation in the Era of Intensive Subsumption: On Political Contestation and Its Consequences.

If this is indeed the paradoxical state of affairs we face today — of trying to account for the first immanentist metaphysics of techno-power — of confronting a nexus-effect of sub-atomizing subjection and cathodic projection, then how are we to proceed from the question of critique to a place of resistance? And how is it that, following the accusations Foucault faced of making no space in his work for a philosophy of subjective resistance, (or at least of a semi-autonomous space of contestation), that the situation can be considered anymore workable today? And how can a viable means of desubjectivation and/or resubjectivation be asserted at the very moment that cultural criticism is undergoing an accelerated phase of intensive subsumption by capital — everywhere perfecting the uninterrupted reproduction of the social sphere to such a degree that we may now face a regime of total subsumption?

And how can new forms of resistance be posited in architectural terms — or through archio-technological interventions that address subjectivation? Does creating a space of resistance still require a material counterpart, i.e., a literal space where resistance can develop — or simply a space for the denaturalization of indo-colonization? And if so, how can this be thought in materialist terms, i.e., as the possibility of a *realpolitik?* How can it be linked to a genealogy of counter-conquest outside of western philosophies of architectural design, or positioned alongside other histories of resistance — premodern, modern or postmodern? Where shall we begin our work when the fourfold diagram of control has become quite comfortable as a lived phenomena and even appears comforting when compared to the Fiberopticism of tomorrow?

Is our question today not already one full hour past the eleventh — an incontestable event of technological appropriation that is finally irreversible, even in its smallest determinations? Or, are techniques of resistance already being enacted all around us — and can we push them a little further towards a tipping point of real consequence? Is there a plausible theoretical counterpart, or any number of theoretical counterparts, to the expression of populace signs of resistance to the fourfold diagram of control and the universalization of capitalist time? And if we can't escape the affective designs of neo-Panopticism, is it finally possible to Feng Shui the Panopticon, i.e., to live differently among its subjective and/or subjectivizing determinations? Or, to cast the same question in a slightly different light, can we develop a counter-metaphysics that challenges not only the biopolitical control of life and death, but the science of apparatuses that mobilizes biopower as a power of *death over life*, i.e., as that which mistakes a living-body for a dead-thing (autopsy-being, cadaver-being, examination-being)? Is there still a means of resisting the ongoing transformation of neo-Panopticism into Fiberopticism — or the advent of a pure, unmitigated Thanatos-politics?

5.8 The Defense of the Body at the Moment of High Antagonism: Resistance to Physical, Financial and Psychic Expropriation.

Quite unreservedly, our answer must always be that resistance is still possible, and that within the moment of the greatest exercise of power, also the most probable! In classic Marxian terms, we might call revisionary Panopticism an instance of intensive contradiction, or an example of high antagonism, or even the interminable acceleration of class warfare — class warfare at a point of terminal velocity where the ongoing socio-economic catastrophe of capitalist rule can no longer be avoided or deferred. Resistance today is defined against crash-course-capitalism, casino-capitalism or what Naomi Klein calls 'disaster capitalism' — a regime that not only operates without regulatory or restrictive division, but which profits through "crisis exploitation", aggressive accumulation, the disintegration of state power(s), the explosion and implosion of debtor states, and the massive transfer of "public wealth into private hands".[132]

With the rise of this kind of 'Shock and Awe' capital, resistance increasingly depends on the defense of the body and an *in-bodied politic*; its spaces of free and anonymous action; its ability to organize and undertake public activities; its protection from immanentist forces and immanent dangers; its potential to withdraw from invasive forms of social inscription, corporeal conscription and judico-legal injunctions. Sometimes this has to do with overcoming the machinations of economic appropriation; sometimes it means contesting physical exploitation; and sometimes it means challenging psychological expropriation — but today neo-Panopticism plays a key role in instituting and maintaining all three of these conditions — it may even be the definitive motif of physical-financial and psychic expropriation, (a fourfold power of control — Synoptic, Banoptic, Bio-optic and Acoustic — based on three forms of economic subsumption, i.e., formal-real-intensive subsumption). If this is indeed the case, then how then are we to proceed?

5.9 Against the Automatic Functioning of Unconscious Forms of Subjectivation: Resistance Beyond the Play of Negativity.

Here we could begin a list of archio-techniques that would help to undermine Panopticism, but such a list would miss the critical aspect of the contemporary context — namely, that techno-Panopticism is itself a place of techniques without end. Instead, our immediate goal must always be the de-reification of consciousness, and particularly, the self-regulating consciousness of control know as Panopticism — or, in this case, the de-reification of hyper-Panopticism understood as the automatic functioning of unconscious mechanisms of subjectivation. Undoubtedly, this seems like an insurmountable task. But such an undertaking, is first of all, a matter of understanding what the task at hand consists of.

In the western world, and especially in liberal democracies, this kind of de-mystification is always posited as being formal, i.e., as the simple undermining of the program(s) of previous generations. Of course, this diagram of 'progress' is everywhere synonymous with the drive of capitalism toward the perpetual overcoming of its own limits. It represents a form of speaking about discrete attenuations in performa, and specifically, about derivations is the historicity of performa, as if subtle shifts in content and form were unprecedented ruptures in the social order (avant-gardism). Such reified forms of engagement make radical politics dependant upon little more than a roundabout definition of 'revolution'; the eternal return of the same as a form of negative involution; or 'progress' posited as infinite negation — even Hegel's bad infinity.[133] This is why today it is important to adopt a model or models of resistance that occur at the inter-section of different forms of synthesis: western and eastern, academic and populace, ancient and modern, etc., etc. But again we find ourselves confronted with the question, where to begin — especially with regard to the geopolitical stage, or what Marx referred to as the 'world historical stage'. This last question will be the guiding theme of our final reflection on the architecture(s) of subjectivation, as well as the leitmotif that brings our medita-tions to a close.

SIXTH MEDITATION

The Futurity of Foucault and Feng Shui

Interestingly, for all his liberal political positions, Bentham was opposed to the American Revolution. In particular, Bentham was a critic of the concept of "inalienable rights", as spelled out in Jefferson's Declaration of Independence. Bentham argued that rights derive from the actions of the government itself and can be taken away by the government. Bentham famously referred to the doctrine of Natural Rights as "nonsense on stilts".[134]

    Gregory Bergman & Peter Archer

Barou: Does the deployment of the Panoptic system pertain to the whole of industrial society? Is it the work of capitalist society?
Foucault: Industrial society? Capitalist society? I have no answer, except to say that these forms of power reoccur in socialist societies: their transposition was immediate.[135]

    Jean-Pierre Barou & Michel Foucault in conversation

...many devoted students and scholars — in China and in the West — are presently contemplating a new name for feng shui in order to draw a dividing line between popular pursuits and fruitful enquiry. Several suggestions have been put forward, with no success other than continuing a long debate on the correct categorization of feng shui.[136]

    Ole Bruun

6.1 Communism, Capitalism and the Reterritorialization of Social Space in the Twentieth Century: Worker Camps and Worker Encampment, (or the Capital-Time of Life).

Two of the most often cited genealogies of social control related to Panopticism in the twentieth century are (1) the institutional bias's of international style in the west and (2) the war against Feng Shui practices in the east, (as well as religion in the broader sense). In no uncertain terms, this reterritorialization of social space allowed instrumental rationality to become the defining motif of architectural interpolation in urban city-centers while also eradicating the last competing systems of belief from the preindustrial/agrarian world. Even though both of these diagrams of power were motivated by the euphoric hope of creating a 'modern' world — a world free of monarchical and tsarist rule — the first of these transformations was valorized through the spread of programmatic manifestos and corporatist ideologies while the second was directly asserted through state sponsored repression. 'Form follows function' and the rejection of ornament found its uncanny double in the notion that the people should follow the party in overturning the religious practices of the orient. And while the ideological divide between the east and the west is not so easily downplayed, it is important to understand how socialist demands and bureaucratic commands were both tied to the dream of a rationally deter-mined and well-controlled society — and perhaps, even more so, to a kind of Panopticism unbound.

In terms of architectural subjectivation, this contest played itself out through the dichotomies of the worker line and the corporate cubical; concrete partitions and glass walls; necessary correction and proper training. One side of the political spectrum came to rely on enforced worker camps while the other developed the full potential of worker encampment (the capital-time of life);[137] one side deployed adjudicated measures while the other focused on measured administration; one relied on unreserved brutality, the other, on protracted conviviality. In the dialectic of achio-subjectivizing antagonisms, communist dictates and capitalist rule where both implicated in fortifying the gaze of unceasing inspection — the first explicitly, the second, implicitly.

And yet, in the final analysis, these diametrically opposed forms of governance proved to be little more than two sides of the same coin — where the (re)production of the regimented body by monopoly powers was the end result of both crony capitalism and party corruption. This unacknowledged trauma of twentieth-century labor, (a trauma defined by forced accommodations), was premised on the need for an incontestable top down chain of command, i.e., literal top down chains of command in corporatist skyscrapers and industrial factories, as well as top down planning by incontestable statist actors. And yet, over time, these two regimes of repression would produce global reaction formations during the later part of the twentieth century that would challenge the Panoptic strictures of communism and the Panoptic structures of capitalism through nothing less than a total revolution.

6.2 The Anti-Panoptic Revolution: Postmodern Architecture and the Return of Feng Shui.

The first of these two counter-Panoptic tendencies is very well known in architectural studies, even becoming the international expression of a kind of anti-modern academicism that has as many different names and mantras as it has styles and practitioners. Whether parading around under the banner of postmodern pastiche, deconstructionist play or simulationist virtuosity, (and much more recently, under the title of neo-baroque exuberance), this wild proliferation of anti-modern architectural forms has come to represent nothing less than a concerted challenge to the rationalist diagram of institutional control initiated by Bentham more than two centuries ago.[138] By comparison, the second sweeping moment of counter-statist conquest has been less sensational, but no less widespread. This is the return of Feng Shui practices as a decidedly populous discourse in both urban and rural life.

But how did either of these revolutions come to pass against seemingly insurmountable odds, and under what terms were the fictions of modernity and modernization brought into unconcealment? And more importantly, why is the axial relation of counter-conquest stratagems associated with anti-modernist architecture and Feng Shui practices of continuing importance today? And how can the valorization of particularity associated with postmodern motifs and post-religious Feng Shui practices be placed under the sign of what Alain Badiou calls the universal exception — or is the idea of producing the universal exception already the anti-modern demand par excellence, i.e., the disruption of a well-controlled world?[139]

6.3 Post-Structuralism, Feng Shui and New Economies of Intuition: The Rise of Double Coded Meanings in Architectural Practice and the Revival of 'Life Techniques' in Architectural Appropriation.

Arising out of the cultural revolutions of the 1960s, post-functionalist attitudes of every kind — toward family, state, sexual relations, work and production in general — gave rise to some of the most sweeping forms of deterritorialization the field of architecture has ever known, especially in the course of a single generation.[140] This occurred through the postmodern integration of 'pure' and populist motifs; deconstructionist impositions and dynamic forms of folding; simulationist strategies and seductive fabrication techniques — or what the architectural theorist Charles Jencks describes as double-coded systems of meaning:

Today I would still partly define Post-Modernism as I did in 1978 as double coding — the combination of modern techniques with something else (usually traditional building) in order for architecture to communicate with the public and a concerned minority, usually other architects. The point of this double coding was itself double. Modern architecture had failed to remain credible partly because it did not communicate effectively with its ultimate users... and partly because it did not make effective links with the city and history.

In spite of its democratic intentions, Modernism had become elitist and exclusivist. At the same time, architects, as any profession in an advanced civilization, have to keep up with highly technical, fast-changing requirements and their professional peers. They are necessarily caught between society at large on the one hand and a very specialized discipline on the other. The only way out of this dilemma is a radical schizophrenia; being trained to look two opposite ways at once. Thus the solution I perceived and defined as post-modern: an architecture that was professionally based and popular as well as one that was based on new techniques and patterns. To simplify, double coding means elite/popular, accommodating/subversive and new/old.[141]

In light of this shifting relationship to architectural practice, we should also ask if Feng Shui is another kind of architectural discipline that is focused on producing double coded meanings — and if the triumph of peoples rights in the west, (the general strike in France, women's liberation, the civil rights movement, etc.), wasn't mirrored by the return of 'the peoples religion' in the east?

Afterall, the first of these new attitudes toward architectural design, or at least the one most readily identified as the postmodernist outlook, worked to undermine the traditional distinctions between high/low culture, austere forms/ commercial motifs, and geometric hermeticism/popular eclecticism.[142] The second new 'school of thought' on architectural appropriation — deconstruction — challenged any clear division between inside and outside, functionalism and artifice, contained and open space, use-value and indeterminacy.[143] The third new dialog on the architectural scene, often called parametricism or any number of new names for folding architecture, focused on upsetting the grid, undoing rationalist planning, undermining architectonic efficiency, and turning structuralist economies of design on their head.[144] The fourth set of new commitments, which was popularized under the moniker of simulationism, made all of the aforementioned relations seem reversible, illusionary and parasitic — inaugurating a type of resistance that moved architectural forms into a realm of virtuality that forced every binary relation to oscillate at the edge of (il)legibility.[145] Yet, the return of Feng Shui practices during this same period could be seen as offering up something of a fifth economy of intuitions — or what the German philosopher Wolfgang Schirmacher calls 'life techniques' — that are decidedly post-structuralist in orientation.[146] From such a perspective Feng Shui can be cast as another radically anti-Panoptic (dis)position because it posits a system of double coated meanings about architectural praxis in being rational about its intuitions, spiritual about its determinations and universal in its application toward fulfilling individual desires.

In this way premodern practices of architectural divination find themselves returned to a place of prominence in the postmodern world and even name its defining ethos, i.e., the reduction of a rigid, functionalist, rational world-view. But what was the outcome of these different architectural revolutions — postmodern, deconstructionist, parametric, simulationist, and Feng Shui-ist, respectively? Are these mixed methodologies miming a fight against the Panopticism of nineteenth century societies of command *rather than* twentieth century economies of control? And if so, do these 'schools' of resistance to archio-discipline still offer us any useful resources for subverting the strict territorialization of subjectivity that issues from revisionary Panopticism today?

6.4 Resistance to Neo-Panoptic Control as a Question of the Destining of Species-Being: The Free Play of Discipline and the Ethical Dimension of Resistance that Exists Behind Our Backs.

The answer here is a yes and a no. Yes, inasmuch as the anti-modern revolutions in architectural practice provide us with an endless catalog of *saying and making-other than* Panoptic forms. No, if one considers the rather formal and commercial projects that have everywhere co-opted these archio-techniques. And yet, quite irrespective of this division between ends and means, the lasting contribution of the counter-modern, (or post-modern), revolution was having demonstrated not only that other paradigms of design and belief were possible, but that they were also socially and economically viable. Some of the great monuments of this period have even become centerpieces of tourism, the arts, education and government. Often disdained by the public at first, many of these same structures now enjoy wide praise and attendance — and even the admiration of a new generation of architects that aim to introduce even greater forms of dynamism into the city skyline than what the twentieth century allowed for.

In the space of a just a few decades, dramatic advances in technology and architectural planning have challenged every preconceived notion of program and style associated with the modern enterprise — or to put it much more simply, they have disrupted the Panoptic regime of visibility as a totalizing effect. While trying not to make too sweeping a generalization, the anti-rationalist impetus behind many of the most notable buildings from last quarter century resulted from an engagement with the world of organic forms — and often with technological facades, blobs and skins, i.e., non-rectilinear motifs. In this regard, early postmodern architecture tended to rely on double coated systems of reference while turn of the century building seems to be dominated by over-coated meanings. This trend is the most detectable where complex regimes of citation and allusion are accentuated by the use of new materials and advanced building techniques. Largely derived from computational schema, auto-poetic intimations and emergent phenomena, this latest mutation in architectural self-reflexivity is probably best described as a polymorphic play of allegorical modes of building that are not so much 'about building' as they are the rhetoric of pleasure, sensuality and dynamism.

Running counter to a great deal of public fanfare, the criticisms lodged against this contagious post-functionalist ethic always seems to circle around the same set of claims: that such buildings only further destabilize any sense of a grounded subject; that they introduce new labyrinths of loss and melancholy into perception; that they further reify a hyper academic relation to form and function that the general public is at pains to understand; and that such architecture only furthers the prospects of capitalist appropriation through an ethic of spectacularization. Worst of all, many anti-modern buildings require complex economies of maintenance, the most objectionable of which are defended on the basis that disposable building can even have 'positive economic effects'.

And while all of the above criticisms are certainly true by degree, these various critiques miss a key point, if not *the key point of the anti-modern revolution.* That while these radical reconfigurations of architectural space were defended as the antidote to western rationalism, (as being anti-Panoptic in every regard), the diagram of control associated with (neo)Panopticism mutated into an appendage/assemblage power that became applicable to almost any kind of architectural affront. In other words, Panopticism managed to keep up with the times, even integrating these programs into its auspicious nature. Ultimately, anti-modern architects fought to overturn the social physics that are produced by Panoptic forms while leaving the question of audio-visual technologies unaddressed. This problematic relationship between the means of social control and different models of architectural practice still defines the terrain of critical interventions in the field of archio-subjectivation today.

And yet, irrespective of these shortcomings, the inheritance of postmodernist, deconstructionist, parametric and simulationist architectures can still provide us with an expansive vocabulary of strategies with which to enact a politics of resistance to neo-Panopticism today — and more specifically, a politics which is not reducible to the logic of supersession, academicism, spectacularization or other forms of démodé reactive nihilism, i.e., infinite negation. However, these various archio-strategies need to be conceived alongside a series of minimal determinations that are directed at subverting (neo)Panoptic power *in-suti*. In this regard, Feng Shui continues to be of the greatest importance, both for its embrace of double coated meanings and its desire for new triangulations of meaning: threefold, fourfold, fivefold, sixfold, etc. Subtracted from its commercial preoccupations — or deployed as a politics of subtraction from the logic of a given world — Feng Shui might even hold the potential for appropriating space in a way that brings the truth of organic life into unconcealment. But here, 'organic life' must be thought of only as enacting a politics of truth to the degree that it subtracts species-being from the bio-politicization of labor and discipline.

Or, to put it another way, the truth of Feng Shui as a political practice rests on being able to puncture a hole in the logic of any world that is circumscribed by Panoptic subjectivation, (personal, cultural, economic or governmental). From such a position, Feng Shui could also be seen as opening onto an ethical dimension of discipline, and archio-discipline in particular, that we have yet to fully perceive. However, this would be something like a kind of discipline that happens when we give free play to our faculties — or an ethical dimension of subjectivation that exists behind our backs — a kind of discipline that happens through *indisciplinary means*.[147] But how can we envision this challenge to archio-Panoptic relations not only as the dissolution of a well controlled world, but also as the production of a world that embraces 'control' as part and parcel of our ethico-subjective becomings — or of ethico-disciplinary practices that inexist within the regime of neo-Panopticism, (askesis, the care of the self, etc.)?

6.5 Political Revolutions in Architectural Space From East to West: Interdisciplinary Social Practices Contra Disciplinary (Statist) Forms.

If postmodernism was the last well-known architectural revolution in the west, then the international and cosmopolitan turn in Feng Shui practices during the second half of the twentieth century represents its populace counterpart from the east. And yet, what few realize today is that the institution of Panoptic forms in communist countries was much more rigorous and uniform than its western manifestations — if however, a bit more didactic. Corporatist and communist imperatives converged on a single programmatic point during high modernism — there were to be no populist motifs outside of corporate logos and party propaganda; no public spaces for creative or artistic expression; and no visible sites for personal or popular sentiments. The big difference being that in communist countries, this also meant outlawing religious motifs and spiritual knowledges, *which included Feng Shui*.

Consequently, the great Feng Shui revival was not just a matter of valorizing harmonious relations, it was and still is, a political revolution in-itself — a fight against enforced illegality in the public sphere. While anti-modern architecture made its appearance in the full light of day, Feng Shui was kept alive by an elite underground of secretive practitioners during the long decades of state sponsored repression. Concealed by a small population of archio-mystics for more than half a century, Feng Shui carried within it a number of nominal political determinations, or even *interstitial motifs*, that allowed people to think about architectural relations differently. And like anti-modern forms of architecture, Feng Shui was divided by any number of disciplinary disjuncture's and different schools of thought, such as the school of Orientations, the school of Forms, the Flying Star school and the Black Hat school. In other words, postmodernism and Feng Shui are both dispersed and highly un-uniform movements — everywhere mixing, sampling and reworking the contributions of the past into post-historical forms of architectural praxis that seek to address the present as a condition that is always already implicated in the *pre*-sent.

6.6 Bio-Politics and Qi: Architectural Revolutions and the Question of Subjective Attunement.

While the noncommercial history of Feng Shui is still not common knowledge in the western world — where it is often associated with favoring curvilinear forms, pleasurable and non-obtrusive color arrangements, the creation of sacred or meditative spaces and the reduction of anxiety and clutter — its practices are actually part of a much longer history of resistance toward state, theocratic and colonial power.[148] In fact, *Feng Shui might be considered one of the great knowledges of the common*, only being divided and subdivided into different schools of thought over the course of the last few centuries. While Feng Shui began to take shape as a distinctive set of practices around the period of 960-1279, (during the Song Dynasty in China), its traditions are actually much older than the moment of its emergence as a 'discipline' of sorts.[149] Originally something more like an ancient form of populist metaphysics — pre-godhead, pre-doctrinal, pre-hierarchical — Feng Shui addressed everything from ancestral influence to grave orientation, cosmology and curing illnesses, diet and numerology, symbolism and architectural relations — for all intents and purposes, nothing was beyond its purview. The only element that tied these disparate concerns together was finding a balanced attunement to the living flow of *qi*, or the worldly energy birthed of the cosmos.

As such, Feng Shui was the first counter-rationalist metaphysics based on the control of everyday effects and actions — and perhaps even, *the first metaphysics to actively address the micro-physics of architectural power*. Largely derived from mixed traditions of fortune telling, folk religion, proto-environmental and community concerns, and even outright superstition, the art of the geomancer was to restore the equilibrium between all things through minor interventions, rituals, numerical calculations, principled design, electromagnetic indicators and personal intuitions. In this regard, the different schools of Feng Shui were, are, and continue to be a means of addressing the notion of an everyday metaphysics, or a nominal metaphysics — one which consists of impersonal forces rather than supernatural beings; that projects an immanent order rather than a 'natural world'; and which defends the value of developing tactical counter-measures to the disciplinary distribution of architectural power.

In this way, many of the contemporary schools of Feng Shui have come to represent a mystico-pragmatic articulation of architectural subjectivation that stands in sharp contrast to the rationalist-transcendental diagram of control associated with (neo)Panopticism. That is Fung Shui's enduring contribution to ages past as well as the reason for its dynamic return to the cultural imaginary of the present. But how are we to think about the resurrection of Feng Shui practices in the pseudo-communist east and the highly commercialized west — especially in relation to the fourfold diagram of power that is extending its operations in every possible direction vis-à-vis globalization? How can a power that was used to undermine the claims of dynastic rule, colonial superiority, communist command and corporatist injunctions be mobilized against the sub-atomizing power of control societies — and what kinds of resources does it present us with today? In other words, how are we to think the critical purchase of Feng Shui in the age of bio-politics?

6.7 Feng Shui as a Profane Vocation: Agamben and the Political Function of Archio-Inoperability, (or the development of indisciplinary practices as a means without end).

Of course the answer here is not at all simple. Feng Shui, like a lot of anti-modern architecture, is pretty indefensible in its current incarnation, i.e., as a system of affective arrangements that are complementary to domestic and corporate incarceration. While Feng Shui has been adopted to streamline the layout of the workplace and the home; and to cut down on mental distractions of every kind; and even to create a sense of neo-spiritual security in some of the most commercial and elite institutions in the world — these are all examples of increasing instrumentalization and the appropriative power of capital. With the rise of post-industrial production, labor time has become co-extensive with domestic life so that work can function unceasingly, i.e., so that domesticity is a secondary concern even in the environment proper to it. This transformation, in many ways, is the result of having naturalized Panoptic assemblages that institute not only a permanent state of visual availability, but also audio-visual and textual communicability, i.e., circumspect availability.

The inverse effect of this transformation of private space is that the workplace has increasingly come to resemble a second home, everywhere incorporating time for recreation, shared meals, corporate counseling, rest and even some basic domestic chores. But this is not just a first world phenomenon. In a far greater number of 'developing' countries, the industrial workplace has been transformed into a home/prison/tenement where outsourced labor is forced to stay 'in-house' at all times with the exception of a few monthly or bi-monthly furlough days to visit family members and friends outside the world of work. With the subsumption of domestic environs by big Capital (transnational capital), co-workers are finally naturalized as familial partners and work-time as the time-of-life.

Within the spectrum of domestic co-option, it is only the wealthiest individuals and most prestigious corporate firms that contract the services of Feng Shui gurus to harmonize the social environment of (re)production. Regrettably, this is the most radical perversion of the counter-Panoptic tradition, often streamlining workflow and *qi* into an uneasy alignment of radical subjection that is opposed to metaphysical speculation and (de)subjectivizing attunement. In order to avoid this impasse, Feng Shui practices must seek out a series of minimal determinations and political commitments that actively address the metaphysics of our times, i.e., the domination of revisionary Panopticism over and against every form of private and/or public space.

In this way, a new revolution in Feng Shui practices — the revolution against the fourfold design(s) of Panoptic power — can only come about through the radicalization of every doctrine heretofore known or associated with the history of Feng Shui. The School of Forms might be made to (re)consider the substantive effects of placement, outlines and structuration in relation to the contours of Neo-Panoptic control; the School of Orientations might be engaged in rethinking the science of watching — its branches and constellations, its possible directions and points of obfuscation, its ability to create a space or spaces of reserve from the omnipresence of audio-visual assemblages, etc., etc.; the School of the Compass might undertake a study of the natural properties of building materials as well as how they can be used to create electromagnetic dead zones and safe zones that defy the logic of (in)security by making new public spaces and private areas for non-surveilled exchange; the School of Changes might undertake an analysis of affective relations of all types and kinds — "directions, elements, colours, functions, people, situations, emotions and more", but with the aim of resisting social control and the reproduction of the hyper capitalist order;[150] the Flying Star School could radicalize our understanding of all forms of modern numerology, (codes, dataveillance, bio-metrics, etc., etc.), in relation to the dictates of credentialism and verification technologies, not to mention developing the means for their possible subversion; and the Black Hat Sect of Feng Shui, which tries to bring all of these elements into a *common relation* through a new vision that is at once "pragmatic and purified (of historical baggage)... focused on buildings, landscape, gardens, colours, interior design, harmonious living and the flow of qi..." could be the first form of neo-organicism to provide a significant challenge to the uninter-rupted power of hyper-Panoptic appropriation by thinking the whole of surveillance beyond the influence of its parts — i.e., to address the question of totality, or really, of resisting a totalizing power.

While these are just a few open-ended examples of what is possible today, one can only imagine what could begin to happen if the concerns of Feng Shui were brought into dialog with postmodern, deconstructionist, folding and/or simulationist practices of architectural resistance in an effort to produce anti-Panoptic forms of (co)habitation. This would be just one sense in which we could Feng Shui the Panopticon, take the Panopticon from behind, or above, or below for that matter, and deterritori-alize its forms of social stratification.

In historical terms, this would mean something like restoring the original meaning of the *Book of Rites* (grave divination) in order to recapture the futurity of resistance from ages long past — to find the gravest terms of revolution buried among the terminology and prejudices of the premodern world — and to align them with the most radical precepts of the architectural present. In this way, the *Book of Rites* could finally be replaced by a new *Book of Rights* (living divination) situated around the demand for privacy and judico-legal protections against the endless cataloging of the body and its corporeal markers. If this seems unimaginable, or just too daunting a task, it is important to remember that only a generation ago the practitioners of Feng Shui rewrote its traditions, *almost in their entirety,* to accommodate the environmental and new age movement(s). Only now we must be willing to go one step further — we must be willing to to challenge neo-Panopticism as the dominant form of biopower within imperial democracy — and this means profaning geomantic metaphysics beyond mere commercialization, environmentalist appropriation or neo-spiritual co-option.

The renowned philosopher of worker camps, excremental being (homo sacer) and (neo)sovereign power, Giorgio Agamben, has described the act of profanation as an operation which returns a thing to 'the common use of men'; as an act which joins the sacred and the profane in an entirely inappropriate relation — that of free play; and as "a special form of negligence, which ignores (the) separation (of the human and the divine), or rather, puts it to a particular use."[151] In applying Feng Shui to a populace agenda, its metaphysical presuppositions have already been greatly diminished. All that is needed now is to return Feng Shui to being a decidedly profane vocation in an effort to "deactivate the apparatuses of power and return to common use the spaces that power had seized" — and spaces of (neo)Panoptic power in particular.[152] But this would mean rejecting its metaphysical basis, its instrumental orientations, and its schematic system of qualifiers in order to create a new poverty of means freed of an obligatory relationship to ends. In this way, profane geomancy could be seen as the cultivation of desubjectivizing effects, i.e., as the valorization of life-practices freed from a "genetic inscription within a given sphere" of biopolitical domination.[153] Taken as a form, or as a series of forms, that actively destabilize hegemonic models of archio-discipline, the profanation of Feng Shui would mean nothing less than the "creation of a new use ... (and the) deactivating of an old use, rendering it inoperative" — or of Panopticism opened toward de-reified forms of concealing and revealing the body socius.[154]

6.8 Disrupting the Field of Terrestrial Magnetism Constituted by the Micro-Physics of Archio-Subjectivizing Power: Feng Shui as a Model of Resistance to (neo)Panopticism.

In this way, the populism of Feng Shui can be joined to the anti-Panoptic urge behind counter-modern architecture, creating an entirely new means of resistance toward neo-Panopticism/neo-imperialism in their contemporary form(s). What has been characterized in the past as an ecological discourse, a spiritualist cosmology and a practical craft can be given a concrete political agenda that is more than the negative definition of resistance offered up by the anti-modern paradigm, (more than mere negation), yet it would only be a positive definition of resistance by degree, *never a positive definition in total*. In this way, the three great traits attributed to Feng Shui by the preeminent scholar of geomantic divination, Ole Bruun, could find their full political relevance by extending (1) the play of an "anti-authoritarian medium of expression ... without systematic form," (2) by valorizing a discipline that acts as "a counterbalance to oneness" (totalizing power) and (3) by developing a post-colonial genealogy of "informed resistance to theocratic/state power" — and especially of state power shot through by the designs of hyper-capital and the theocratic/sovereign rule of neo-Panopticism.[155]

This would constitute a provisionary coda of minimal deter-minations that could inform anti-Panoptic practices within the worlds of architecture and design. Such a dynamic synthesis of revolutionary cartographies — mystic and postmodern, populace and theoretical, eastern and western — would produce ever new and evolving strategies of 'terrestrial magnetism' that actively seek to disrupt the physics of social control associated with the fourfold diagram of archio-audio-visual power. In practical terms, profane geomancy could be something like an indisciplinary branch of Feng Shui studies that attempts to understand social control in its sub-atomizing forms, i.e., as a materialist topology of lived experience that is both superstructural and super-(un)natural; highly stratified and perceptually (in)dividuated; concrete and radically immaterial. In this way, architectural relations can be reconfigured to secure the rights of the body over and against the fourfold assemblages of revisionary Panopticism. We might even be able to say, that through such means, the despotic regime of neo-Panopticism can be dissembled.

6.9 Nietzsche, Heidegger, Schirmacher: The Rise of Neo-Panopticism and the End of Metaphysics.

Of course, here I say dissembled *rather than* disassembled because dissemblance is our greatest means of resistance today — i.e., of making socio-economic relations appear other than they are; of showing how archio-power operates and how to subvert its means; of drawing new diagrams and new cartographies of exchange that make a space for social relations outside of Panoptic structures and capitalist strictures. To reinvent the practice of Feng Shui against neo-Panopticism means trying to think governmentality and (in)security within a universalized Panopticon differently than what it is — and also, as other than what it threatens to become (Fiberopticism). Of course, this is also another way of saying that we both have to accept and disavow the consequences of modernity. Accept: that advances in modern warfare, biological warfare, travel and technology have made the necessity of surveillance an irreversible part of our common life world. Disavow: that this means we must all live in a state of permanent pre-criminal suspicion.

But to disavow such a state of affairs is also not enough — we must attempt to produce new relations that make the existence of unsurveilled zones not only possible but also quite practical. The ability to speak freely in the truest sense of the word; to gather together without evidence of natural or artificial record; to exist without the threat of being perpetually subjected to new and increasingly invasive measures of inspection — this must be our common destination, or at least, our means of defending what defines the common today as a literal space of resistance. Such a trajectory could be thought of as a demand to secure different forms of (de)subjectivation; to follow the hope of a truly democratic future; or as a *realpolitik* based on fortifying the constitutional rights of liberal society against its illiberal tendencies.

Failing this means forfeiting democracy for (in)security, or being forced to inhabit a hyper-dialectics of social control that is animated by socio-economic precariousness and hyperactive methods of screening, cataloging and detaining subjects. Or, failing Nietzsche, it means that God returns in the form of an all-seeing, all-hearing and all-knowing Fiberopti-*con* — the literal possibility of extracting sense-data from fibrous being.[156] Or, to put it in Heideggerian terms, we might finally come to live in the age of completed metaphysics not because metaphysics has come to an end but because metaphysics is finally enforce without end — an auto-adjudicated electro-metaphysics, (metaphysics commuted from the technological enframing of being to the invasive *in*-framing of being, i.e., indo-colonization).[157] Or, as Wolfgang Schirmacher has pointed out, there is even a much more foreboding conclusion to the era of metaphysics, one that is rooted "in the finite nature of human existence", where "when the world as we perceive it, has reached its end", along with the "extinction of the human species", that alone will be "the proof of the death of metaphysics."[158]

To place the prospects of such a shift alongside the rise of control societies, one has to first understand the rise of Neo-Panopticism as a reaction-formation to the decline of metaphysical control and belief — where "the end of metaphysics means that the lifelong project of the human species has become in its historical development a suicidal enterprise."[159] From such a perspective, control societies are little more than a real dead-end — a means of allowing for the *extinction of the many at the high cost of preserving the few, (archiodisciplinary genocide).*

6.10 From Common Use to a Politics of the Common: Rethinking Feng Shui as a Bio-Political Practice.

Instead of this deplorable destining, imagine instead that we only have to take the Foucaultian notion of the care and mastery of the self seriously — and that the spread of Feng Shui practices is already one attempt to do just that. Imagine that resistance means seeking to extend any and every form of critique to neo-Panoptic control — many of which are already well underway all around us. Imagine that populist pleasures and academicism really aren't that far part — and that a real postmodern-populism still awaits us. Imagine that another revolution in Feng Shui practices is just on the horizon as it was only a generation ago — but with a greater sense of urgency and (post)historical necessity. Imagine even, that the east and the west are not really so far apart anymore — that the world grows smaller and more interconnected with each passing day — and that everywhere, people have already begun the work of developing new modes of inhabiting public and private space than what our contemporary forms of constitutional democracy and communist rule provide for. Imagine that Feng Shui is revealed to be what it once already was — *a means without end* — the free play of intuition(s) that existed prior to the determinations of metaphysical power. Imagine that profaning an entire historical tradition, (one more than a millennium old), could open up the possibility of discovering a 'pure use' of discipline — especially a type of discipline that could never posses a determinate set of subjectivizing properties or practices. Imagine that Feng Shui could become a school of thought that "lays bare the true nature of property" and proprietary rights — and even elicit practices of observation, appropriation and exploitation, (the becoming-property of people).[160] Imagine that this kind of revaluation of values can be joined to a politics of the common and that "the profanation of the unprofanable is the political task of the coming generation" — or, more properly, the task of a common generation.[161]

If you can entertain the possibility of this kind of transformation of the global space of resistance, then you might be willing to admit that many different forms of subjectivation are possible outside of what the fourfold diagram of control permits — or rather, entertains. And for those who take up this charge — that such a shift may not only be possible but even probable — than the promise that we can still learn to live together differently, may yet be fulfilled. The messianic force of capitalist antagonism may give rise to a different kind of community; a common community; a community yet-to-come; and even a community of what Giorgio Agamben calls 'whatever-singularities' — a term that signals our generic belonging and desire to be free such as we are, and not as we are intended to be (control-being).[162]

Maintaining a fidelity to resisting revisionary Panopticism in the age of completed metaphysics means holding to the idea that criminalization is not the future destination of all persons, places and public spaces. Rather, if neo-Panopticism serves to teach us anything, it is most decidedly that for which it was not intended: that even though we may have to learn to live as everyday criminals, we might also live by another name — everyday revolutionaries.

Endnotes

1   Massimo De Angelis, *The Beginning of History: Value, Struggle and Global Capital* (London: Pluto Press, 2007) 195.

Prolegomenon to Six Meditations on the Architecture of Subjectivation.

2   Michel de Certeau, *The Practice of Everyday Life* (Los Angeles: University of California Press, 1984) 48.

3   Michel Foucault, *Power*/Knowledge: *Selected Interviews & Other Writings, 1972-1977* ed. Colin Gordon (New York: Pantheon Books, 1980) 59.

4   Ibid. 59.

5   While the term dispositif is not easily translated into English outside of its reference to having an effect on disposition, settlement and territory, I am here referring to the Deleuzian definition of the term as being something like an apparatus. Deleuze sums up the term dispositif in the following way: "First of all, it is a skein, a multilinear whole. It is composed of lines of different natures. The lines in the apparatus do not encircle or surround systems that are each homogenous in themselves, the object, the subject, language, etc., but follow directions, trace processes that are always out of balance, that sometimes move closer together and farther away. Each line is broken, subject to *changes in direction*, bifurcating and forked, and subjected to *derivations*. Visible objects, articulable utterances, forces in use, subjects in position are like vectors or tensors. Thus the three main instances Foucault successively distinguishes — Knowledge, Power and Subjectivity — by no means have contours that are defined once and for all but are chains of variables that are torn from each other." Gilles Deleuze, *Two Regimes of Madness: Text and Interviews 1975-1995* (New York: Semiotext(e), 2006) 338.

6   Foucault has described the mirco-physics of power in the following way: "He who is subject to the field of visibility, and who knows it, assumes responsibility for the constraints of power; he makes them play spontaneously upon himself; he inscribes in himself the power relation in which he simultaneously plays both roles; he becomes the principle of his own subjection." Michel Foucault, *Discipline and Punish: The Birth of the Prison* (New York: Vintage Books, 1977) 202-203.

7   Bruun has characterized the westernization of Feng Shui practices as related to four major shifts: "First of all, it was *amputated* by excluding everything relating to graves (*yin* dwelling), while focusing entirely on houses and homes (*yang* dwelling). Second, it was *de-spirited* in the sense that the workings of the gods, ghosts and ancestors tended to be excluded, while focusing only on impersonal forces. Third, it was to a large extent, *taken indoors*, concentrating on interior design and decoration more than external, physical surroundings. Last, but not least, it was *infused with new concepts*, including ecology, environment, nature and design." Ole Bruun, An *Introduction to Feng Shui* (New York: Cambridge University Press, 2008) 158.

8   Or, we could say that Feng Shui is an instance of anticathexis that aims to repress the hyper Panopticism of the present, *especially as a rationally administrated force of Ego interference.*

9   "The basic thinking is that all elements of our environment have an effect on our physical, emotional and spiritual wellbeing. Crucial are the natural light in our rooms, the colour of our walls, the style and shape of furniture and ornaments and the presence of living plants. Thus, different arrangements of the home and decoration will affect the movement of *qi* and ultimately affect our personal *qi* or wellbeing..." Ole Bruun, *Introduction to Feng Shui,* (New York: Cambridge University Press, 2008) 160.

10   The idea of 'governmentality' is here is used in the

Foucaultian sense as consisting of a series of applied techniques through which a political body reproduces subjects that maintain, secure and defend the social order, while Feng Shui serves as an example of practices that exceed the judicio-legal realm proper — or to put it in Hardt and Negri's terms, the difference between biopower and biopolitics is here re-inscribed under the signs of governmentality (Panopticism) and Feng Shui respectively.

11 Foucault variously described the "arts of existence" in the following way: "those intentional and voluntary actions by which men not only set themselves rules of conduct, but also seek to transform themselves, to change themselves in their singular being, and to make their life into an *oeuvre* that carries certain aesthetic values and meets certain aesthetic criteria." Michel Foucault, *The Use of Pleasure. The History of Sexuality: Volume Two* (Middlesex: Penguin, 1992) 10, 10-11.

12 While Bruun gives many examples of the Berkeley connection, one of the most notable is "Hong-key Yoon, a young Korean who came to Berkley as a student of cultural geography in 1971... Originally serving as an account of Korean and Chinese geomancy for a Western readership, his work clearly reflects the point in time when it was written. Beyond developing the assumption that fengshui is closely related to the natural environment, he defines the art as 'a unique and comprehensive system of conceptualizing the physical environment which regulates human ecology by influencing man to select auspicious environments and to build harmonious structures (i.e., graves, houses and cities) on them'." Ole Brunn, *Fengshui in China* (Honolulu: University of Hawai'i Press, 2003) 339-340.

13 "Foucault describes his philosophical activity not as a form of accumulating knowledge but as a kind of exercise — an *askesis*. This word *askesis* can be misleading. As Foucault assures us in many places, it does not necessarily mean the

practice of self-denial... in the original Greek context it always had a positive and productive meaning — exercising meant perfecting oneself, developing ones capacities, becoming who one is. It referred to physical training in athletics as well as spiritual training, this is, philosophy. Thus, *askesis* is for Foucault... an exercise of thought, a work of thought upon itself." Edward F. McGushin, *Foucault's Askesis: An Introduction to the Philosophical Life* (Evanston: Northwestern University Press, 2007) xiii.

14 Foucault claims that this type of work was expressed in the transformation of an individual's behavior through the alteration of penalties, the revision of these alterations in line with rehabilitation, the use of work and socialization, the 'education' of the prisoner, the supervised and specialized coordination of moral instruction, and the institution of a system of disciplinary measures. See Foucault, *Discipline and Punish*, 269-270.

15 Heidegger has described the 'fundamental characteristic(s) of dwelling' as 'sparing', 'freeing' or bringing 'peace', i.e., to be "preserved from harm and danger, preserved from something, safeguarded." It is here that a Heideggerian reading of Panopticism would be essential in confronting the radical disjuncture between the idea of setting free into the dwelling of being and of escaping the Panoptic eye that watches from the earth and the sky. Martin Heidegger, *Basic Writings: Revised and Expanded edition*. ed. David Farrell Krell (San Francisco: Harper Collins, 1993) 351.

16 The media theorist Norman Klein has described 'scripted spaces' as "a walk-through or click-through environment, (a mall, a church, a casino, a theme park, a computer game). They are designed to *emphasize* the viewer's journey — the space between — rather than the gimmicks on the wall. The audience walks into the story. What's more, this walk should respond to each viewer's whims, even though each step

along the way is prescripted (or should I say preordained?). It is gentle repression posing as free will." Norman Klein, *The Vatican to Vegas: A History of Special Effects* (New York: The New Press, 2004) 10-11.

17 Even though one may speak of a masculine gaze, a feminine gaze, etc., etc., the gaze is always conceived of as the totality of effects that construct a subject — or the totality of the visible field for which a subject becomes *a subject of (re)presentation.* To say that the gaze is made up of different sets of gazes, or that it is decomposable into a series of qualifiable subsets isn't entirely true, and yet, with the advent of hyper-Panopticism it is necessary to understand the construction of the gaze in both its *intensive* and *extensive* dimensions. The hyper-Panoptic gaze is produced by a number of different forces, each of which requires a different kind of accounting for, and investigation into, its means of capture and local determinations.

18 Lacan characterizes the gaze as what "is presented to us only in the form of a strange contingency, symbolic of what we find on the horizon, as the thrust of our experience, namely the lack that constitutes castration anxiety", i.e., the relation to the other and the big Other. Jacques Lacan, *The Four Fundamental Concepts of Psychoanalysis: The Seminar of Jacques Lacan, Book XI* (New York: W.W. Norton & Company, 1998) 72-73.

19 See Arthur C. Clarke, *Profiles of the Future: An Inquiry into the Limits of the Possible* (New York: Harper and Row, 1984).

20 Foucault grants normalizing power five distinctive operations: "it refers individual actions to a whole that is at once a field of comparison, a space of differentiation and the principle of a rule to be followed. It differentiates individuals from one another, in terms of the following overall rule: that the rule be made to function as a minimal threshold, as an average to be respected or as an optimum toward which one

must move. It measures in qualitative terms and hiearchizes in terms of value the abilities, the level, the 'nature' of individuals. It introduces, through this 'value-giving' measure, the constraint of a conformity that must be achieved. Lastly, it traces the limit that will define difference in relations to all other differences, the external frontier of the abnormal (the 'shameful' class of the Ecole Militaire). The perpetual penalty that transverses all points and supervises every instance in the disciplinary institutions compares, differentiates, hiearchizes, homogenizes, excludes. In short, it normalizes." Today, we may have to say instead that the desire for perfected and/or distorted subjects, refers individual actions to *no whole*, where the absent totality of comparison is missing because there is already too much modulated sameness (de-differentiation). In such a scenario irregularity comes to replace difference, or rather, it represses the emergent qualities of difference through the spread of banal particularities. It consists of a system of radically mitigated hierarchies, which produce the affect of uniqueness *within the same, or of variation by repetition, or even of dissimilitude by verisimilitude.* Lastly, contemporary forms of capitalism and neo-Panopticism not only define uniqueness by defect, but they make the irregular into a value in-itself, (a thing to be tracked, bought and sold). In such a scenario, falling out of the social order of the same, or 'the norm', becomes the precondition of a perverse kind of homogeneity — a homogeneity of one(s). Foucault, *Discipline and Punish*, 183.

21 It is worth noting that with the rise of the new economy of image control, invisibility has become one of the key terms for radical politics, especially in the wake of the arrests and imprisonment of the *invisible committee* and members of groups like *Anonymous* and or *wiki-leaks*. We can even imagine a time where invisibility becomes a crime, *if this is*

not already the case today.

22 The three great scholars of contemporary Panic-opticism are undoubtedly Arthur Kroker, Marilousie Kroker and David Cook. This is perhaps, best evidenced in their co-authored work *Panic Encyclopedia: the definitive guide to the postmodern scene.* In a rather amazing passage, the Kroker's and Cook provide a timely diagnosis of our current cyber bureaucracy as a chromatic panic event where: "Parodying the reversibility of the earth's magnetic field, all cyber-bureaucracies are infinitely reversible. Indeed, as bureaucracies spread across the postmodern world, *they assume the characteristics of the magnetic field* (my emphasis). At any point, a sign change may occur, occasioned by transformations in the energy level, by internal political struggles, or by invasion from without. That is, cyber-bureaucracies are subject to the multiplicative 'minus one' rule. Given an arbitrary rule, dictum or state, all judgments, rules, and values can be instantly reversed by the application of the -1 operator. Similarly, all actions and operators can be reversed and resignified *definitionally.* No longer the Orwellian rewriting of history under an ideological guise, the alterity of bureaucratic decisions, like any switching process, requires the couplet, on/off, denial/approval, to sustain its rationality and to maintain the circulability of relational power. Hyper-nominalism is the ruling epistemology of cyber-bureaucracy." Not only is the conversion to thinking of postmodern space as a process of *social ionization* described here in full, but hyper-nominalism was certainly the modus operandi of the Bush administration, with its chromatic alerts to activate a Panic-optic populace and the general reversibility and commutability of its terms — now red, now green, now orange alert; a blanket threat, a general threat, a coordinated threat and so on and so forth. Through such means, Panic-opticism and Pan-opticism become mutually reinforcing

directives — or even complementary drives toward activating the optic capacities of a population in total. Arthur & Marilouise Kroker, David Cook, *Panic Encyclopedia: the definitive guide to the postmodern scene* (New York: St. Martin's Press, 1989) 62-63.

FIRST MEDITATION: Neo-Panopticism and the Disciplinary Order of Neo-Liberal Societies.

23 David Murakami Wood, 'Beyond the Panopticon: Foucault and Surveillance Studies', *Space, Knowledge and Power: Foucault and Geography*, ed. Jeremy W. Crampton and Stuart Elden (Burlington: Ashgate Publishing Limited, 2010) 251.

24 Michael Hardt & Antonio Negri, *Empire* (Massachusetts: Harvard University Press, 2000) 318-319.

25 William Bogard, *The Simulation of Surveillance: Hypercontrol in telematic societies* (New York: Cambridge University Press, 1996) 47.

26 See Thomas Mathiesen, "The Viewer Society: Michel Foucault's Panopticon Revisited." Theoretical Criminology 1 (2) (May, 1997) 215-34, and Didier Bigo, "Globalized (in)Security: The Field and the Ban-optic." *Terror, Insecurity and Liberty: Illiberal Practices of Liberal Regimes After 9/11*, ed. Didier Bigo & Anastassia Tsoukala (New York: Routledge, 2008) 10-48, and David Lyon, "An Electronic Panopticon? A Sociological Critique of Surveillance Theory." Sociological Review 41 (4), (New York: Wiley-Blackwell, 1993) 653-678.

27 In the Foucaultian genealogy of western power, classical forms of justice are defined by the power of inquisition, modern justice by the power of the examination and postmodern power by the expansion of surveillance, yet the "power of the norm appears through the disciplines" developed throughout the course of the eighteenth and nineteenth centuries. Michel Foucault, *Discipline and Punish: The Birth of the Prison* (New York: Vintage Books, 1977) 184.

28 Originally called the Panacousticon, this recently rehabili-
    tated idea of Athanasius Kircher included "long conduits
    linking rooms that are far apart, huge funnels whose vast
    opening cover entire courtyards, and intricately branching
    systems for listening in which are acoustic companion pieces
    to Jeremy Bentham's Panopticon of 1790..." See Siegfried
    Zielinski, *Deep Time of the Media: Toward an Archaeology of
    Hearing and Seeing by Technical Means* (Massachusetts: MIT
    Press, 2006) 182.

29 Jeremy Bentham, *The Rational of Punishment* (New York:
    Prometheus Books, 2009).

30 See, Oscar H. Gandy Jr. "Quixotics unite! Engaging the
    pragmatists on rational discrimination." *Theorizing
    Surveillance: The Panopticon and Beyond*, ed. David Lyon
    (Portland: Willan Publishing, 2006).

31 'Trending' and 'emotional branding' are two sides of the
    same coin, *one locates the consumer in space and time,* the other,
    through the emotional specificity of the buying experience. While
    many advertising consultants now preach about thinking
    spatiality — from utilizing big billboards and key time slots
    to smaller targeted and time based performa, *this is really a
    falsehood.* We are, at every level, a space-time culture that
    seeks to locate the available 'space of the consumer' as well
    as 'the time of consumption, participation and acquisition,'
    — largely as a means to market to each person effectively,
    and even singularly. See Marc Gobé, *Emotional Branding: The
    New Paradigm for Connecting Brands to People* (New York:
    Allworth Press, 2009), and *Thomas H. Davenport & John C.
    Beck, The Attention Economy: Understanding the New Currency
    of Business* (Massachusetts: Harvard Business School Press,
    2001), and B. Joseph Pine II & James H. Gilmore, *The
    Experience Economy: Work is Theater & Every Business a Stage*
    (Massachusetts: Harvard Business School Press, 1999), and
    Bernd H. Schmitt, *Experiential Marketing: How to Get*

Customers to Sense, Feel, Think, Act, Relate to Your company Brands (New York: The Free Press, 1999).

SECOND MEDITATION: The Micro-physics of Class Subjectivation.

32 Jeremy Bentham, *The Rational of Punishment* (New York: Prometheus Books, 2009) 66-67.

33 Michel Foucault, "The Meshes of Power", *Space, Knowledge and Power: Foucault and Geography*, ed. Jeremy W. Crampton and Stuart Elden (Surry: Ashgate Publishing, 2010) 156.

34 Tiqqun, *This Is Not a Program* (Los Angeles: Semiotext(e) Intervention Series, 2011) 175.

35 David Lyon, *The Electronic Eye: The Rise of Surveillance Society* (Minneapolis: University of Minnesota Press, 1994) 62-63.

36 Bentham's texts are permeated throughout by a kind of rationalism ad absurdum, such as the following: "In matters of importance everyone calculates. Each individual calculates with more or less correctness, according to the degrees of his information, and the power of the motives that actuate him, but all calculate. It would be hard to say that a madman does not calculate." Ibid. Bentham, *The Rational of Punishment*, 75.

37 One of Foucault's most concise passages on the micro-physics of Panoptic power is the following: "it can constitute a mixed mechanism in which relations of power (and knowledge) may be precisely adjusted, in the smallest detail, to the processes that are to be supervised; it can establish a direct proportion between 'surplus power' and 'surplus production'. In short, it arranged things in such a way that the exercise of power is not added on from the outside, like a rigid, heavy constraint, to the functions it invests, but is so subtly present in them as to increase their efficiency by itself increasing its own point of contact. The panoptic mechanism is not simply a hinge, a point of exchange between a

mechanism of power and a function; it is a way of making power relations function in a function, and of making a function function through those power relations." Ibid. Foucault, *Discipline and Punish*, 206-207.

38 Bentham characterized the function of 'Panoptic reform' in the following way: "Under the safeguard of continual inspection, without which, success is not to be expected, the Penitentiary House described, includes all the causes which are calculated to destroy the seeds of vice, and to rear those of virtue." But to speak of neo-Panopticism and auto-attunement is to speak about an instrument that brings itself into social accord with its surroundings — *not instrumental rationality but instrumentalized sociality.* Jeremy Bentham, *The Rational of Punishment*, 281.

39 Ibid. Foucault, *Discipline and Punish*, 201-202.

40 Kevin D. Haggerty, "Tear down the walls: on demolishing the panopticon." *Theorizing Surveillance: The Panopticon and Beyond*, ed. David Lyon (Portland: Willan Publishing, 2009) 29.

41 "In short, Foucault's discourse is a mirror of the power it describes. It is there that its strength and its seduction lie, and not at all in its 'truth index', which is only its letimotiv: these procedures of truth are of no importance, for Foucault's discourse is no truer than any other. No, its strength and its seduction are in the analysis which unwinds the subtle meanderings of its object, describing it with a tactile and tactical exactness, where seduction feeds analytical force and where language itself gives birth to the operation of new powers. Such is the operation of myth, right down to the symbolic effectiveness described by Lévi-Strauss. Foucault's is not therefore a discourse of truth but a mythic discourse in the strong sense of the word, and I secretly believe that it has no illusions about the effect of truth it produces. That, by the way, is what is missing in those who follow in Foucault's

footsteps and pass right by this mythic arrangement to end up with the truth, nothing but the truth.

The very perfection of this analytic chronicle of power is disturbing. Something tells us — but implicitly, as if seen in a reverse shot of this writing too beautiful to be true — that if it is possible to talk with such definitive understanding about power, sexuality, the body, and discipline, even down to their most delicate metamorphosis, it is because at some point *all this is here and now over with*. And because Foucault can only draw such an admirable picture since he works at the confines of an area (maybe a 'classical age', of which he would be the last great dinosaur) now in the process of collapsing entirely. Such a configuration lends itself to the most dazzling display of analysis just before its terms have been recalled." Jean Baudrillard, *Forget Foucault* (New York: Semiotext(e), 1987) 10-11.

42 This is the dimension of Panoptic power that Bentham overlooks in being too much of a pragmatist rather than a strict idealist. For Bentham, profit was simply "the prevention of crimes" and the use-value of prison labor for profit was defined in the following way: "It costs little to shoot a man; but everything which he might be made to produce, is lost; and to supply his place with a productive labourer must now be converted into an unproductive one." At every turn, even when it seems obvious, Bentham is unable to radicalize his thesis to reflect the traditional categories of political economy. Instead, he always stops short of thinking 'value' in all of its possible determinations. Effective moral correction and improvement through punishment, training and labor remain the ultimate horizon of Bentham's investigations — not economic enfranchisement *but* moral improvement. The economic for Bentham is just an added selling point to the uniqueness of his inventions. Ibid. Bentham, *The Rational of Punishment*, 66,

79-80.

43 "Surveillance thus becomes a decisive economic operator, both as an internal part of the production of machinery and as a specific mechanism in disciplinary power. 'The work of directing, superintending and adjusting becomes one of the functions of capital, from the moment that the labour under the control of capital becomes cooperative. Once a function of capital, it (now) requires special characteristics' (Marx, *Capital, Vol. I,* 313)". This brief citation by Foucault alludes to the operative context under which (neo-)Panopticism functions — namely, the greater the need for cooperation, *the greater the designs of control.* In our own time however, even this Panoptic presupposition has come into contradiction because post-industrial capitalism limits the possibilities of extensive and intensive cooperation. Ibid. Foucault, *Discipline and Punish,* 175.

44 Foucault is closest to drawing out such a conclusion when he points out how Panopticism is designed to designate mad/sane, dangerous/harmless, and normal/abnormal, but he quickly falls back on describing it in naturalist rather than class terms: "one finds in the programme of the Panopticon a similar concern with individualizing observation, with characterization and classification, with the analytic arrangement of space. The Panopticon is a royal menagerie; the animal replaced by man, individual groupings by specific groupings and the king by the machinery of furtive power. With this exception, the Panopticon also does the work of a naturalist." Ibid. 203.

45 Jacques-Alain Miller already noted this long ago in attributing a supreme utilitarian value to Panopticism whereby "everything must be usable, must work toward a result... all use must be recouped... a life devoid of leisure... In fact, more labor is what Bentham proposes as the purpose of distracting from labor... the panoptic ideal is to achieve

the integral subjection of nature to the useful. Some way must be found to fit even the most basic needs into the profit system." And yet, Bentham's super-usable world is only just realized today — in the world of hyperbolic exchange — where all production is based on overproduction and overcapacity. In such a world neo-Panopticism becomes the inheritance of instrumental rationality redefined as the unlimited extension of technocracy. Jacques-Alain Miller, "Jeremy Bentham's Panoptic Device." October 41, Summer (Cambridge: MIT Press, 1987) 7.

46 Toshimaru Ogura, "Electronic government and surveillance oriented society." *Theorizing Surveillance: The Panopticon and Beyond,* ed. David Lyon (Portland: Willan Publishing, 2009) 272.

47 Ibid. 273.

48 Ibid. 274.

49 Ibid. 274.

50 Ibid. 275-276.

51 Ibid. 277.

THIRD MEDITATION: The Crisis of Capitalist Control at the End of History.

52 Jacques Derrida, *Spectors of Marx: The State of the Debt, the Work of Mourning & the New International* (New York: Routledge, 1994) 77-78.

53 Giorgio Agamben, *Infancy and History: On The Destruction Of Experience* (New York: Verso, 1993) 109.

54 István Mészáros, *The Structural Crisis of Capital* (New York: Monthly Review Press, 2010) 69-70, 72, 81.

55 A term originally coined by Paul Virilio to describe the "synchronization of emotions" and the "globalization of affects", indo-colonization has also come to represent the transvaluation of false consciousness into (Panoptic) hyper-consciousness, over-sensitization, radical stimulation and

infomatic saturation. Indo-colonization is an over-whelming effect constituted by the unrelenting force of electro-affectual devices. In short, it is a new standard in class-based subjection that threatens to take on global proportions. Paul Virilio, *The University of Disaster* (Massachusetts: Polity, 2010) 49, 49.

56 Jeremy Rifkin describes the change from material to immaterial production in the following way: "In an era of property and markets steeped in material values, being omnipresent was a godlike goal. Being able to inflate one's physical presence by expropriating as much material existence as possible is what every propertied person yearned for. It was indeed, to quote Madonna, 'a material world'. The new era, by contrast, is more immaterial and cerebral. It is a world of platonic forms; of ideas, images, and archetypes; of concepts and fictions. If the people of the industrial era were preoccupied with expropriating and reshaping matter, the first generation of the Age of Access is far more interested in manipulating mind. In the era of access and networks, where ideas are the grist for commerce, being all-knowing is the god-like goal. To be able to expand one's mental presence, to be universally connected so as to affect and shape human consciousness itself, is what motivates commercial activity in every industry." Jeremy Rifkin, *The Age of Access: The New Culture of Hypercapitalism, Where All of Life is a Paid-For Experience* (New York: Penguin Putnam, 2001) 54.

57 Ibid. Foucault, *Discipline and Punish*, 170.

58 Ibid. 170.

59 Gilles Deleuze, "Postscript on Societies of Control", *Rethinking Architecture: A reader in cultural theory.* ed. Neil Leach (New York: Routledge, 1997) 311.

60 Ibid. 311.

61 See Richard Florida, *The Rise of the Creative Class... and how*

it's transforming work, leisure, community & everyday life (New York: Basic Books, 2002) and Richard Florida, *The Flight of the Creative Class: The New Global Competition for Talent* (New York: Harper Business, 2005).

62   Zygmunt Bauman, *Liquid Modernity* (Massachusetts: Polity, 2000) 8.

63   Ibid. Deleuze, 309.

64   For Jameson, cognitive mapping represents "a gap, (or) a rift between existential experience and scientific knowledge..." which does not mean that something is "unknowable but merely that it is unrepresentable." Above all else, it is a strategy that enables "a situational representation on the part of the individual subject to that vaster and properly unrepresentable totality which is the ensemble of society's structure as a whole." Fredric Jameson, *Postmodernism, or The Cultural Logic of Late Capitalism* (Durham: Duke University Press, 1999) 52, 51.

65   Baudrillard had already diagnosed this problem in the 1990s by developing the notion of fractal capitalism: "For after the natural, commodity, and structural stages of value comes the fractal stage. The first of these stages had a natural referent, and value developed on the basis of a natural use of the world. The second was founded on a general equivalence, and value developed by reference to the logic of the commodity. The third is governed by a code, and value develops here by reference to a set of models. At the fourth, the fractal (or viral, or radiant) stage of value, there is no point of reference at all and value radiates in all directions, occupying all interstices, without any reference to anything whatsoever, by virtue of pure contingency. At the fractal stage there is no longer any equivalence, whether natural or general. Properly speaking there is no law of value, merely a sort of *epidemic of value*, a sort of general metastasis of value, a haphazard proliferation and dispersal of value." The

problem with such an analysis is that our current contradictions are not based on the 'pure contingency' of value but on
the diminished potential of neoliberal capitalism to be self-
sustaining. Baudrillard's observations should not be read as
a metaphor, but as a real historical stage based on hyperbolic
fractalization in banking practices. If anything, it is a
concrete metaphor for the contingency of trying to generate
value at the point of total systemic contradiction. Jean
Baudrillard, *The Transparency of Evil: Essays on Extreme
Phenomena* (New York: Verso, 1993) 5.

66 Out of Benjamin's four traits of capitalism — (1) that
"capitalism is a purely cultic religion," (2) that it is a cult of
"permanence" where "each day commands the utter fealty of
each worshipper," (3) that the cultic aspect of capitalism
"makes guilt pervasive" and (4) that "God must be hidden
from it and may only be addressed when his guilt is at its
zenith" — only this last condition finds itself changed by the
neo-Panoptic order. In the era of subjectivizing capital, God
need not be addressed at all because God is finally lost
among the details; presenced only by the omniscient act of
watching; and everywhere consecrated and imbibed in the
production and reproduction of the capitalist order itself. In
such a scenario God is finally without proper subjects to bare
witness to the spread of his guilt or lack of remorse.
Subjectivizing capital is unrepentant capital — *Capital beyond
good and evil, or at least equitable proportionality*. Walter
Benjamin, *Walter Benjamin Selected Writings: Volume 1: 1913-
1926* (Massachusetts: The Belknap Press of Harvard
University Press, 1996) 288, 288, 288, 288, 289.

67 Ibid. Foucault, 170.

68 Ibid. Deleuze, 312.

69 "The physical economy is shrinking. If the industrial era was
characterized by the amassing of physical capital and
property, the new era prizes intangible forms of power

bound up in bundles of information and intellectual assets. The fact is, physical products which for so long were a measure of wealth in the industrial world, are dematerializing." Jeremy Rifkin, *The Age of Access: The New Culture of Hypercapitalism Where All of Life is a Paid-For experience* (New York: Penguin Putnam Inc., 2001) 30.

70　Massimo De Angelis has provided perhaps the most succinct reading of how market capitalism, (as it is defined by Hayek), and Panopticism work together to secure disciplinary order. The originality of his analysis lies in understanding how a supposedly 'open' or 'emergent' order (market capitalism) is entirely compatible with a restricted one (Panopticism). For Massimo, this convergence of interests can be summed up in eight key points: "1. Origins. The 'planner plays an important role in the design of the *parameters* of the order/mechanism. 2. Impersonality and efficiency. The impersonal mechanism of coordination of individual subjectivities (plans) is functional to the maximisation of extraction of labour (Bentham) or maximisation of efficiency (Hayek). 3. Extension and integration. The order/mechanism can be generalized through the social field by means of the modular properties of the panopticon (Bentham) or commodification of new areas of life. 4. Imperfect knowledge. There is the recognition that power (inspectors in Bentham's panopticon or the state in Hayek's market) has imperfect knowledge of individual plans. 5. Freedom of *private*, not social, individuals. The order/mechanism relies on freedom of private individuals (*given* a menu). The consequent strategic intent of power is the emphasis on co-optation of unintended consequences of individual freedom. 6. Role of 'enclosures'. Individual confinement is a *condition* of individual freedom. In Bentham, the confinement is created by the cell's walls, while in Hayek it is created through property rights, which turn individuals into private individuals. 7. Disciplinary order. The mechanisms of coordination (watchtower or competition) distributes punishments or rewards and is 'invisible' to individuals. In Bentham, this is the power behind the watchtower, in Hayek it is the emergent and ongoing compulsion of the competitive process. 8. Fetishism and signaling. Both mechanisms function through 'shadowy projections' of real life activities. In the panopticon these are the light signals, in the competitive market these are price signals." While De Angelis's reading of "the striking similarities and complementarities between Hayek's and Bentham's systems" is essential to understanding how control societies function, his conclusion that it leads to a "fractal panopticon" of interrelated virtual inspection houses diminishes the different types and kinds of 'inspection', 'correction' and 'emulation' that have come to dominant society at large. The fourfold design of social control, defined by the terms Synopticism, Banopticism, Bio-opticism and the Acousticon, delineate the need to confront the post-historical condition of hyperbolic social conditioning rather than a singular fractal logic (Panopticism). Here, Massimo makes the mistake of providing us with a false analogy by superimposing a thesis about the 'natural' order onto the social order. Such a perspective assumes the premise of nearly mechanical actors conditioned by a self-replicating system rather than showing how social automatism develops out of a plurality of control mechanisms. Massimo De Angelis, *The Beginning of History: Value Struggles and Global Capital* (London: Pluto Press, 2007) 207, 206, 216.

71   Semio-capital is a term used by Christian Marazzi to describe how "the chain of production has, in fact, become a linguistic chain, a semantic connection, in which communication, the transmission of information, has become both a raw material and an instrument of work, *just like electricity* (my

emphasis)." In other words, affective capital is something that flows through us — it is not imposed on the social order from the outside but reworks social being from the inside through the appropriation of language, emotions and communicative drives. Christian Marazzi, *Capital and Language: From the New Economy to the War Economy* (Los Angeles: Semiotext(e), 2008) 50.

72 Of course, Marx's famous passage from 'The Historical Tendency of Capitalist Accumulation' is of the greatest importance here. Not only have all the conditions which would allow for 'the expropriation of the expropriators' come to pass, but *they may very well be passing us by*. The mass consolidation of production, the spread of socialized labor, the growth of international markets, and even the barrier of profitability under the (hyper)capitalist mode of production have all, quite arguably, been reached — but the "integument is (yet) burst asunder." By all accounts, this is what the institution of affective capital aims to prevent. What Marx could never have foreseen however, was that consciousness, affections and emotions would also be expropriated, slowly dismantling not only class consciousness *but individual consciousness as well*. The 'expropriation of the expropriators' is now just as likely as the prolonged spectacularization of viral forms of value and even tautological systems of valorization — the production of a grand edifice of unconscionable forms of hyper motivated consumption. This is the blind spot of a great deal of Marxist discourse today, and of the work of Hardt and Negri in particular. Biopower finds itself bound by the destructuration of revolutionary consciousness tout court. Karl Marx, *Capital, Volume: I* (England: Penguin Books, 1990) 929.

73 While Hardt and Negri have probably gone the furthest of any of the neo/post-marxians in trying to describe the (pre)conditions of social revolution today, their definition of

biopolitics is often too abstract, relegating the bios to being a "a power of life to resist", as well as the event of freedom and productive "innovation" — or, much more closely in line with Deleuze, as the power to "create a new world". If we take their thesis to its conclusion in saying that "The biopolitical event, in fact, is always a queer event, a subversive process of subjectivization that, shattering ruling identities and norms, reveals the link between power and freedom, and thereby inaugurates an alternative production of subjectivity", we still must ask how is this to be accomplished, and not necessarily as a series of prescriptions but as a question of theoretical injunctions and qualifiers, such as freedom from what? Which ruling identities and norms? And is it still even the 'norm' which must be resisted? While Hardt and Negri often relate social revolution to pragmatic ends in resisting "all forms of metaphysical substantialism or conceptualism" it is the concrete identification of subjectivizing process which is often absent from their texts, i.e., *Panopticism*. Michael Hardt and Antonio Negri, *Commonwealth* (Massachusetts: Harvard University Press, 2009), 57, 61, 61 62-63, 63.

74 István Mészáros has provided us with perhaps the most succinct definition of intensive subsumption to date: "Capital, when it reaches a point of saturation in its own setting and, at the same time, cannot find outlets for further expansion through the vehicle of imperialism and neo-colonialism, has no alternative but to make its own indigenous labor force suffer the grave consequences of the deteriorating rate of profit. Accordingly, the working classes of some of the most developed 'post-industrial' societies are getting a foretaste of the real viciousness of 'liberal' capital." István Mészáros, *The Structural Crisis of Capital* (New York: Monthly Review Press, 2010) 86-87.

75 Ibid. 312.

FOURTH MEDITATION: The Fourfold Science of Subjectivation as a System of Apparatuses.

76 Judith Butler, *The Psychic Life of Power: Theories in Subjection* (Stanford: Stanford University Press, 1997) 83.

77 Michel Foucault, *Power/Knowledge: Selected Interviews & Other Writings 1972-1977* (New York: Pantheon Books, 1980) 56.

78 Kirstie Ball, "Organization, surveillance and the body: toward a politics of resistance." *Theorizing Surveillance: The Panopticon and Beyond*, ed. David Lyon (Portland: Willan Publishing, 2006) 299.

79 See Thomas Mathiesen, "The Viewer Society: Michel Foucault's Panopticon Revisited." Theoretical Criminology 1 (2) (May) 215-34.

80 How Debord described the function of the spectacle — that it "unites what is separate, but (that) it unities it only *in its separateness*" — has taken on a completely new meaning for us today. For Debord, the radical homogeneity of alienated social actors was the effect of spectacularization. Yet today, the estrangement of being *too much the same* is itself a condition of *codified difference* — the fatalistic production and commodification of 'one-offs' — customized products sorted, sifted and projected to an audience of (in)dividuals hoping to capture the last traces of subjective fulfillment vis-à-vis personalization. Guy Debord, *The Society of Spectacle* (New York: Zone Books, 2002) 22.

81 Norman Klein has described the hummingbird effect in the following way: "Then a hummingbird stops in front of my window. The wings resemble a ferocious little automaton. It is modernity incarnate, except for a fundamental problem. The hummingbird is not moving at all. It is so fast that it is standing still. We fly ahead at such intense speeds that in fact, we are standing still, like an e-mail from Antarctica, like a movie trailer edited so fast, you no longer see any places

within the story, just a blur of action." Klein's description of cultural meta-stability continues along the same lines in asserting that: "We fly to another continent, but find the same ten stories waiting there. Even eerier, the airport back home has been shipped to a foreign city. Maybe the tanker jets can do that. What's more, this airport was restocked in route. Now it sells foreign newspapers. Otherwise it feels mostly the same... Along with shipping the airport from one continent to another, globalization brought ten thousand varieties of repetition, more games about infinite choice based in a world of absolute predestination." Norman M. Klein, *Freud in Coney Island and Other Tales* (Los Angeles: Otis Books/Seismicity editions, 2006) 97, 97.

82 David Lyon, *Surveillance after September 11* (Malden: Polity Press, 2003) 48.

83 Dider Bigo, "Globalized (in)security: the field and the ban-optic." *Terror, Insecurity and Liberty: Illiberal practices of liberal regimes after 9/11,* ed. Didier Bigo and Anastassia Tsoukala (New York: Routledge, 2008) 45, 45.

84 "All significant concepts of the modern theory of the state are secularized theological concepts, not only because of their historical development — in which they were transferred from theology to a theory of the state, whereby, for example, the omnipotent God became the omnipotent lawgiver — but also because of their systematic structure, the recognition of which is necessary for a sociological consideration of these concepts." Carl Schmitt, *Political Theology: Four Chapters on the Concept of Sovereignty* (Chicago: University of Chicago Press, 2005) 36.

85 In attempting to do what Carl Schmitt roundly avoided, Agamben has tried to provide a theory of 'the state of exception' in relation to public law, which is undoubtedly the most obscure condition of constitutional dictatorship. While the state of exception is something like a legal injunction that

cannot have a properly legal form, Agamben has revealed its seventeenth century bias's by noting that "the state of exception appears as a threshold of indeterminacy, between democracy and absolutism." This too, is how the fourfold diagram of control and the deployment of Banopticism appears in our contemporary moment. Giorgio Agamben, *State of Exception* (Chicago: University of Chicago Press, 2005) 3.

86   Ibid. Bigo, 44.

87   David Lyon, *The Electronic Eye: The Rise of Surveillance Society* (Minneapolis: University of Minnesota Press, 1994) 60.

88   Ibid. 66.

89   Ibid. 70, 65.

90   Ibid. 75.

91   Here I am referring to the famous passage on ideology where Althusser says that the "interpellation of hailing... can be imagined along the lines of the most commonplace everyday police (or other) hailing: 'Hey, you there!'" Only with electronic Panopticism, we are really speaking about a silent form of hailing, inceptual hailing or the subconscious call of auto-affiliation and/or social accommodation. See Louis Althusser, *On Ideology* (New York: Verso, 2008).

92   Here I am taking enterterpellation to mean those things which enter the body and its private environs; which invest its organs and its psychological states; and which circumscribe the home and other places of private repose. No one need be 'hailed' by institutional control in an era of 'institutionalized' subjectivity, inferrogatory apparatuses and enterrogatory discipline. Afterall, with the rise of an immanentist metaphysics there is no institutional call proper, i.e., no authoritative guarantor.

93   Mark Poster, *The Mode of Information: Poststructuralism and Social Context* (Chicago: University of Chicago Press, 1990) 72.

94   Ibid. 91, 87.

95   "In addition to an advanced technology (whose capacities were discussed at the outset of this chapter) and a disciplined self-surveillant populace, the Superpanopticon imposes a new language situation that has unique, disturbing features. The electronic information gathering that constitutes databases, for all its speed, accuracy and computational power, incurs a tremendous *loss* of data, or better, imposes a strong reading on it. Contemporary surveillance in databases relies upon digital as opposed to analog recording of information. It is a language of zeros and ones combined into great complexities but still deriving from that simple grid. Digital encoding makes no attempt to represent or imitate and this is how it differs from analog encoding." Mark Poster, *The Mode of Information: Postructuralism and Social Context* (Chicago: University of Chicago Press, 1990) 94.

96   Jeremy Rifkin has described LTV in the following way: "When businesses talk about letting go of the idea of selling products one at a time to as many customers as possible and, rather, concentrating on establishing a long-term relationship with each individual customer, what they're really focusing on is the potential of commodifying a person's entire lifetime of experiences. Marketing specialists use the phrase "lifetime value" (LTV) to emphasize the advantages of shifting from a product-oriented to an access-oriented environment, where negotiating discrete market transactions is less important than securing and commodifying lifetime relationships with clients." Jeremy Rifkin, *The Age of Access: The New Culture of Hypercapitalism where all of life is a paid-for experience.* (New York: Penguin, Putnam Inc, 2001) 98.

97   Marx has described the move from formal subsumption to real subsumption in the following terms: "The general

features of the formal subsumption remain, viz. *the direct subordination of the labour process to capital,* irrespective of the state of its technological development. But on this foundation there now arises a technologically and otherwise specific mode of production — capitalist production — which transforms *the nature of the labor process and its actual conditions.* Only when this happens do we witness *the real subsumption of labour under capital...* the real subsumption of labour under capital is developed in the forms evolved by relative, as opposed to absolute surplus value... capitalist production now establishes itself as a mode of production sui genesis and brings into being a new mode of material production." Karl Marx, *Capital Volume I* (New York: Penguin Books, 1990) 1034-1035.

98 "The process we are describing here is not merely formal: it is material, and it is realized in the biopolitical terrain. The virtuality of action and the transformation of material conditions, which at times are appropriated by and enrich this power to act, are constituted in ontological mechanisms or apparatuses beyond measure. This ontological apparatus beyond measure is an expansive power of freedom, ontological construction, and omnilateral dissemination..." or "Today labor is immediately a social force animated by the powers of knowledge, affect, science and language... this notion of labor as the common power to act stands in a contemporaneous, coextensive, and dynamic relationship to the construction of community. This relationship is reciprocal such that on the one hand the singular powers of labor continuously create new common constructions, and, on the other hand, what is common becomes singularized. We can thus define the virtual power of labor as a power of self-valorization that exceeds itself, flows over onto the other, and, through this investment, constitutes an expansive commonality. The common actions of labor, intelligence,

passion, and affect configure a *constituent power*." Michael Hardt and Antonio Negri, *Empire* (Cambridge: Harvard University Press, 2000) 357-358.

99 Ibid. 96.

100 Giorgio Agamben has provided an acute reading of the rise of bio-metricism and the potential it holds for releasing us from the strictures of familial belonging *or* our cultural heritage by reducing all life to "naked life", vis-à-vis the identification of the self with only its biological markers. However, for Agamben, biometrics also erases the ethic gap between a subject and the mask of persona by directly identifying a person with their biological make-up. Agamben sees the downside of this same social equation as contributing to "a general collapse of the personal ethical principles that have governed Western ethics for centuries" by disassociating the notion of identity from the achievements attributed to an individual. Whichever perspective one chooses, Agambem is certainly at his best when he says that "the more the citizens of the metropolis have lost intimacy with one another, the more consoling the virtual intimacy with the apparatus becomes (an apparatus that has learned in turn to look deeply into their retinas). The more they have lost all identity and all real belonging, the more gratifying it has become for them to be recognized by the Great Machine..." This is, of course, a wonderful description of the denatured relations that are engendered by neo-Panopticism today. Giorgio Agamben, *Nudities* (Stanford: Stanford University Press, 2011) 52, 52, 53.

101 Bio-power is variously defined by Foucault as the power over life, or the power to administer and produce life along two poles: "One of these poles — the first to be formed, it seems — centered on the body as a machine: its disciplining, the optimization of its capabilities, the extortion of its forces, the parallel increase of its usefulness and its docility, its

integration into systems of efficient and economic controls, all this ensured by the procedures of power that characterized the *disciplines: an anatomo-politics of the human body.* The second, formed somewhat later, focused on the species body, the body imbued with the mechanics of life and serving as the basis of biological processes; propagation, births and mortality, the level of health, life expectancy and longevity, with all the conditions that can cause these to vary. Their supervision was effected through an entire series of interventions and *regulatory controls: a bio-politics of the population.*" While Foucault describes these processes as "starting in the seventeenth century, today, the term bio-power takes on its full meaning in being the power to reproduce, reduce or deny life — as a means of destructuration, deregulation and liquidation — as a way of heightening class conflict and social antagonisms and even as a power of obfuscation, erasure and exile. Michel Foucault, *The History of Sexuality, An Introduction: Volume I* (New York: Vintage Books, 1990) 139, 139.

102 See Kim Zetter, "Anonymous Hacks Security Firm Investigating It: Releases E-mail." *Wired* http://www.wired.com/threatlevel/2011/02/anonymous-hacks-hbgary/ (accessed Feb 5th, 2011, 5:50pm).

103 Dörte Zbikowski, "The Listening Ear: The Phenomena of Acoustic Surveillance" *CTRL SPACE: Rhetorics of Surveillance from Bentham to Big Brother,* ed. Thomas Y. Levin, Ursula Frohne & Peter Weibel (Massachusetts: MIT Press, 2002) 35.

104 Ibid. 35.

105 Of course, the other plausible alternative to such a twist of events is that Batman chooses to mirror the judico-legal means of the state apparatus, deciding that Panacousticism *is* ultimately the most effective means of eliminating his criminal targets. Upon further reflection, he discretely requests that Lucius or his replacement extend its capabil-

ities for future capers. This is the ending implied by Batman taking the blame for the fall of a lost figure of justice (Harvey Dent) — a gesture that only further obscures the literal and figurative two-faced position of today's protectionist polices.

FIFTH MEDITATION: Social Control Between Panopticism and Fiberopticism.

106 Michael Hardt & Antonio Negri, *Empire* (Massachusetts: Harvard University Press, 2000) 331-332.

107 Maria Los, "Looking into the future: surveillance, globalization and the totalitarian potential." *Theorizing Surveillance: The Panopticon and Beyond*, ed. David Lyon (Portland: Willan Publishing, 2009) 90-91.

108 Jacques-Alain Miller, "Jeremy Bentham's Panoptic Device." October 41, (Summer) 5.

109 Merriam-Webster On-line, http://www.merriam-webster .com/dictionary/totalitarianism. (accessed August 17, 2011, 4:30pm).

110 Ibid. Los, 71, 72, 76, 76, 75, 83.

111 Ibid. 75.

112 In other words, revisionary Panopticism is that paradoxical condition of power that doesn't need to unify its operations in order to consolidate its effects. Instead, it pulls together its mechanisms of control through various apparatus's, assemblages, networks and the like that remain separate until specific conditions call for a re-articulation of its means and modal connections.

113 Ibid. Los, 83.

114 Whether we defer to the section on 'Estranged Labor' from the *Economic Manuscripts of 1844* or 'Machinery and Modern Industry' from *Capital Volume I*, it is quite clear how far away we are from the conditions of production that were first analyzed by Marx. We now need a fuller history of alienated production that can account for immaterial as well as

material forms of labor and which doesn't take private property as its point of departure, but begins instead with the expropriation of consciousness from the bio-cycle of organic labor. Of course, Marx is closest to this when describing the intensification of work between day labors to secure their jobs over and against increasing mechanization as well as one another. Today, this scenario finds its fullest expression in the post-industrial marketplace, where the worker medicates him or herself to adjust to (1) the hyperbolic pace of labor, (2) increasing social competition, (3) the precariousness of employment, (4) the heightened demand for credentialism and (5) the opening of the home to workplace activities.

115 Much like the way Lyotard described Mademe Edwarda's madness, which stems from "excessively enjoying her profession" as a prostitute, Hyperbolic capital depends on eroticizing the great ephemeral skin of production, i.e., of producing affects and *even an excess of affects* (jouissance), at the site of exchange. Jean-Francois Lyotard, *Libidinal Economy* (Indianapolis: Indiana University Press, 1993) 140.

116 Lyotard describes the libidinal economy of socio-economic pulsions as a system of "tensor signs: (where) each thing and part-thing being on the one hand a term in a network of significations which are unremitting metonymic referrals, and indiscernibly, on the other hand, a strained singularity, an instantaneous, ephemeral concentration of force." Ibid. 69.

117 Jean Baudrillard, *The Illusion of the End* (Stanford: Stanford University Press, 1992) 27.

118 Ibid. 27.

119 Ibid. 27.

120 "Hegel remarks somewhere that all facts and personages of great importance in world history occur, as it were, twice. He forgot to add: the first time as tragedy, the second as

farce." Karl Marx, *The 18th of Brunmaire of Louis Bonaparte* (New York: International Publishers, 1998) 15.

121 Here I am alluding to Benjamin's reading of historical materialism as a form of historicity who's "basic principle is not progress, but actualization." Walter Benjamin, "Re: Theory of Knowledge, Theory of Progress", *Benjamin: Philosophy, Aesthetics, History,* ed. Gary Smith (University of Chicago Press: London, 1989) 47.

122 Slavoj Zizek, *Violence* (New York: Picador, 2008) 34. See also, Alain Badiou, *Logics of Worlds: Being and Event II* (New York: Continuum, 2009) 444.

123 Here I am referring to Gilles Deleuze's reading of the Leibnizian soul: "Leibniz constructs a great baroque montage that moves between the lower floor, pierced with windows, and the upper floor, blind and closed, but on the other hand resonating as if it were a musical salon translating the visible moments below into a sound above." Gilles Deleuze, *The Fold: Leibniz and the Baroque* (Minneapolis: University of Minnesota Press, 1993) 4.

124 Paul Virilio, *The University of Disaster* (Malden: Polity Press, 2010) 34-35.

125 Michael D. Mehta has noted the way in which "Nanotechnology is stimulating advances in surveillance and monitoring technology. By facilitating the miniaturization of remote camera technology, the panoptic effects from surveillance become magnified. It will soon be possible to place undetectable video cameras, microphones and transmitters anywhere one wishes". This of course, includes the interior of the body (indo-colonization). Michael D. Mehta, "On Nano-Panopticism: A Sociological Perspective." http://chem4823.usask.ca/cassidyr/OnNano-Panopticism-ASociologicalPerspective.htm, (accessed August 15th, 2011, 1:13pm) 2.

126 Electro-convulsive control resembles *sovereign discipline* in

relying on a model of physical torture. Nano-technologies make the examination of *disciplinary subjects* an issue of pure interiority or enterrogatory conjecture. Op-technical discipline relies on the desire to make the subject confess before a higher power. Gene-therapy relies on the futurity associated with *mystical regimes* of control. The organ-trade is the latest update in modern disciplinary eugenics and corporeal expropriation. Taken together, these new diagrams of control might finally displace Panopticism as the reigning ethos of post-historical subjectivation.

127 Maxime Ouellet has described the global effects of cybernetic capital in the following terms: "The subject of cybernetic capitalism is thus distinguished from the autonomous modern subject in that rather than defining itself by its reflexive capacity to act upon its external world, it does so by its ability to self-regulate according to the information received from its environment. The individual defines him or herself by a capacity to adapt, since in cybernetics all beings are defined by the nature of the information exchanges they maintain with their environment (Wiener 1961). Understanding the spectacle in terms of governmentality means that it also entails governing at a distance: that is, it entails a technique that atomizes individuals and encloses them within their own private space in ways that engender their adaptability in relation to capital's requirements... This process of subject formation occurs for states as well as individuals. A new set of knowledges, specifically that of benchmarks, has emerged by which states can be compared and compare themselves in relation to this 'new beauty contest'. For example, the Network Readiness Index, a measuring tool developed through collaboration between the Institut Européenne des Affaires, the World Bank and the World Economic Forum, aims to determine the countries in which the introduction of ICTs presents the greatest

profitability potential. Another index, the Anholt-GMI Nation Brand Index presents itself as the primary analytic tool allowing the measurement of each country's power in step with a series of criteria founded on perceptions of 'global public opinion' as far as cultural, political, human, commercial, and investment potential of the states trademarks are concerned.

The 'branding' practice of companies and individuals is thus extended to the state, aiming to commodify its attributes with the goal of attracting capital and qualified labor in an information society... Cybernetic capital and its logic of spectacular governmentality blur the conceptual categories upon which modernity was founded. State and enterprise, public and private, media and market, citizens and consumers seem to converge in a permanent, networked, global system." Maxime Ouellet, "Cybernetic capitalism and the global information society: From the global panopticon to a 'brand' new world." *Cultural Political Economy*, ed. Jacqueline Best and Matthew Paterson (New York: Routledge, 2010) 190-191.

128 What Horkheimer and Adorno postulated in their analysis of the culture industry, (which here is posited under the name of Synopticism), is but one function in the contemporary diagram of control: "The most intimate reactions of human beings have become so entirely reified, even to themselves, that the idea of anything peculiar to them only survives in extreme abstraction: personality means hardly more than dazzling white teeth and freedom from body odor and emotions. That is the triumph of advertising in the culture industry: the compulsive imitation by consumers of cultural commodities which, at the same time, they recognize as false." Such an analysis now looks tame, or even perversely comforting, when compared to the regime of Technoptic control. Today, let us give this proclamation about ends and

means rationality a final Foucaultian twist: Homo-vigilare is the real 'end of Man'. Max Horkheimer and Theodor W. Adorno, *Dialectic of Enlightenment: Philosophical Fragments* (Stanford: Stanford University Press, 2002) 136.

129 While Haraway's "Cyborg Manifesto" was one of the greatest contributions to post-essentialist Feminism, it now reads like classic American positivism — a perspective best summed up in the concluding line "I would rather be a cyborg than a goddess." Donna J. Haraway, *Simians, Cyborgs and Women: The Reinvention of Nature* (New York: Routledge, 1991) 181.

130 Here I am referring to state imposed laws about reproductive rights and population control in select Pacific rim countries. In this regard, the J-horror films are all allegorical tales about the intrusion of bio-power into familial life.

131 In *The Disappearance of Childhood* Neil Postman provides a reading not only of the 'new norm' of control societies — "the adult-child" or the infantilized-adult — but also a reading of how the erasure of childhood goes hand in hand with a dramatic rise in childhood crime. Sadly, this rather recent development only furthers the supposed need for expansive Panoptic control throughout society as a whole. In many ways the plight of Carol Ann and Samara are represented in this double movement, both living lives that feel overlooked by adult's forgetting their parental duties, as well as children forgetting to participate in the life of childhood. To quote Postman: "All the foregoing observations and inferences are, I believe, indicators of both the decline of childhood and a corresponding diminution in the character of adulthood. But there is also available a set of hard facts pointing to the same conclusion. For example, in the year 1950, in all of America, only 170 persons under the age of fifteen were arrested for what the FBI calls serious crimes, i.e., murder, forcible rape, robbery, and aggravated

assault. This number represented .0004 percent of the under-fifteen population of America. In that same year, 94,784 persons fifteen years or older were arrested for serious crimes representing .0860 percent of the population fifteen years or older. This means that in 1950, adults (defined here as those over and including fifteen years of age) committed serious crimes at a rate of 215 times that of the rate of child crime. By 1960, adults committed serious crimes at a rate 8 times that of child crime; by 1979, the rate was 5.5 times. Does this mean that adult crime is declining? Not quite. In fact, adult crime is increasing, so that in 1979, more than 400,000 adults were arrested for serious crimes, representing .2430 of the adult population. This means that between 1950 and 1979, the rate of adult crime increased threefold. The fast-closing difference between the rates of adult and child crime is almost wholly unaccounted for by a staggering rise in child crime. Between 1950 and 1979, the rate of serious crimes committed by children increased 11,000 percent! The rate of nonserious child crimes (i.e., burglary, larceny, and auto theft) increased 8,300 percent." Therein perhaps, is part of the answer to why neo-Panopticism has been univer-salized today, not only because child and adult crime have both been on the rise for over half a century but because the other name for the rise of the adult-child as a 'normative construct', (or even of the modulated (in)dividual proper), is finally, the society of infant-terribles — *a criminally infan-tilized population*. Neil Postman, *The Disappearance of Childhood* (New York: Vintage books, 1992) 99, 134.

132 Naomi Klein, *The Shock Doctrine: The Rise of Disaster Capitalism* (New York: Picador, 2007) 11, 18.

133 For Hegel, "the bad infinite is through and through a beyond, never anything present." Or, to put it somewhat differently, it is "the mere negation of something." For Hegel this is a problem for the properly synthetic moment because

it removes phenomenal reality from the flow of time, i.e., becoming. In turn, this abstraction of experience is a problem for cognition because it induces a degree of unreality into the idea and its determinations, which are never stable. For our concerns, this is problematic because the work of the negative is often synonymous with capital overcoming its own limitations. We return to Hegel not so much to address the historical condition, but to try to add a concrete dimension to our multiplicitous post-historical becomings, i.e., to adopt a radically duplicitous perspective on the concrete dialectic(s) of historical becomings. Georg Wilhelm, Friedrich, *Lectures in Logic* (Indianapolis: Indiana University Press, 2008) 106, 109.

SIXTH MEDITATION: The Futurity of Foucault and Feng Shui.

134 Gregory Bergman & Peter Archer, *I watch therefore I am* (Avon: Adams Media, 2011) 120.

135 Michel Foucault, *Power/Knowledge: Selected Interviews & Other Writings, 1972-1977* ed. Colin Gordon (New York: Pantheon Books, 1980) 160.

136 Ibid. Bruun, *An Introduction to Feng Shui*, 194.

137 If Agamben is able to say that today "it is not the city but rather the camp that is the fundamental biopolitical paradigm of the west" this is not only because the camp is defined as a space where the state of exception begins to become the rule, but because post-industrial labor is itself defined by the state of exception vis-à-vis unending crisis, unlimited hours, perpetual precariousness, etc. Labor under hyperbolic capital is constituted by so many extreme situations — where the 'control man' of labor is slowly transformed into the corporate muselmann. Giorgio Agamben, *Homo Sacer: Sovereign Power and Bare Life* (Stanford: Stanford University Press, 1998) 181.

138 Here, I am following the work of Charles Jencks in positioning the shift from Modern to Postmodern architecture as a battle caught somewhere between the Newtonian world and the world of emergent properties and processes. As Jencks says in *The New Paradigm in Architecture*: "in the sciences and in architecture itself a new way of thinking has indeed started. It stresses self-organizing systems rather than mechanistic ones. It favors fractal forms, self-similar ones, over those that are endlessly repeated. It looks to the notions of emergence, complexity and chaos science more than to linear, predictable and mechanistic sciences. In more technical terms it is based on non-linear dynamics, and a new worldview coming from contemporary cosmology. From this perspective it sees our place in a universe that is continuously emerging, as a single creative unfolding event. This event is very much an activity, something that has been going on for about thirteen billion years, an affair that contains us in its narrative... this is one of the great insights of our time to be celebrated in architecture as in all the arts." Charles Jencks, *The New Paradigm in Architecture* (New Haven: Yale University Press, 2002) 1.

139 For Alain Badiou the universal exception, or really the universality of the exception, is what "constitutes a hole in knowledge." It is a singular event "which, although identifiable as a procedure at work in a situation, is nevertheless subtracted from every predicate description. Thus the cultural traits of this or that population are particular. But that which, traversing these traits and deactivating every registered description, universally summons a thought-subject, is singular." Alain Badiou, *Theoretical Writings* (New York: Continuum, 2004) 143, 144.

140 Charles Jencks describes the same change in the following way: "Post-Modernism as a cultural formation started... at many points and times. It grew up with the counter-culture

of the 1960s, the rise of the post-industrial society first in America, the disenchantment with Abstract Expressionism in the art world, the growth of a global market and so on. By contrast, the First World War, Hiroshima and the Holocaust are all markers that philosophers and historians have seen as turning points, as creating the crisis of modernity. In architecture, the case can be made that the shift occurred when modern architecture became mass-cult, the historic city was threatened by economic forces, and architects rediscovered architectural DNA, that is, the continuity of languages and historic types. This rediscovery created its own formal crisis." Charles Jencks, *The New Paradigm in Architecture* (New Haven: Yale University Press, 2002) 55.

141 Charles Jencks, *What is Postmodernism?* (West Sussex: Academy Editions,1996) 29-30.

142 Perhaps the best summation of the Postmodern outlook in architecture is still to be found in the opening lines of Robert Venturi's *Complexity and Contradiction in Architecture*, and especially in those few short paragraphs from Nonstraightforward Architecture: A Gentle Manifesto: "Architects can no longer afford to be intimidated by the puritanically moral language of orthodox modernist architecture. I like elements which are hybrid rather than 'pure', compromising rather than 'clean', distorted rather than 'straightforward', ambiguous rather than 'articulated', perverse as well as impersonal, boring as well as 'interesting', conventional rather than 'designed', accommodating rather than excluding, redundant rather than simple, vestigial as well as innovating, inconsistent and equivocal rather than direct and clear. I am for messy vitality over obvious unity. I include the non sequitur and proclaim the duality.

I am for the richness of meaning rather than the clarity of meaning; for the implicit function as well as the explicit function. I prefer 'both-and' to 'either-or', black and white, and sometimes grey, to black and white. A valid architecture evokes many levels of meaning and combinations of focus; its space and its elements become readable and workable in several ways at once." Robert Venturi, *Complexity and Contradiction in Architecture* (New York: the Museum of Modern Art, 1966) 16.

143 Charles Jencks has characterized the rise of Deconstructionist Architecture in the following way: "If there really is a 'Neo-Modern' architecture, as many architects and critics have been quick to claim, then it must rest on a new theory and practice of Modernism. The only such development to have emerged in the last twenty years — known as Deconstruction or Post-Structuralism — takes Modernist elitism and abstraction to an extreme and exaggerates already known motifs, which is why I would continue to call it 'Late'. But it also contains enough new aspects which revalue the suppositions of cultural Modernism to warrant the prefix 'Neo', 'New' or 'Late' — it *is* a matter of debate, and of whether the emphasis is on continuity or change: but the fact of a Deconstructionist movement in architecture has to be accepted. Reflecting changes in the literature of the 60s (Roland Barthes' 'death of the author' and, later, 'pleasures of the text') and change in philosophy (Jacques Derrida's notion of critical 'deconstruction' and *'différance'*), the movement has been most comprehensively developed by Peter Eisenman as a theory and practice of negativity (*'not*-classical', *'de*-composition', *'de*-centering', *'dis*-continuity')". Charles Jencks, "Deconstruction: The Pleasures of Absence." *Deconstruction in Architecture* (New York: St. Martin's Press, 1988) 17.

144 Greg Lynn has reflected back on rise of folding architecture as the third movement after postmodern complexity and Deconstructionist tendencies in the following way: "As I

argued in the original *Folding in Architecture* essay, since Robert Venturi and Denis Scott Brown's influential *Complexity and Contradiction in Architecture* (1966), it has been important for architecture to define compositional complexity. Ten years ago, the collected projects and essays in the first edition of this publication were an attempt to move beyond Venturi's pictorial collage aesthetics and the formal and spatial collage aesthetics that then constituted the vanguard of complexity in architecture, as epitomized by Johnson and Wigley's 'Deconstructivist Architecture' exhibition at MoMA in 1988. The desire for architectural complexity in both composition and construction continues today and can be characterized by several distinct streams of thought, three of which have connections to the projects and arguments first laid out in the Architectural design issue of *Folding in Architecture*: voluptuous forms, stochastic and emergent processes, and intricate assemblages." Greg Lynn, "Introduction." *Folding in Architecture*, (Great Britain: Wiley-Academy, 2004) 9.

145 This last form of architecture has been described by Neil Leach as displaying an obscene fascination with excess, overcapacity, saturation, stimulation and hyper-real experience. It is a type of architecture that creates a lack of meaning in a culture of hyper-reification, where the play of affects supplants structures of meaning *and even the play of meaning* — it is an architecture of anesthetizing effects — or of unmitigated simulationist virtuosity. See Neil Leach, *The Anaesthetics of Architecture* (Massachusetts, MIT Press, 1999).

146 Wolfgang Schirmacher has described life techniques, or what I am referring to with regard to Feng Shui as *living divination*, in the following way: "Today, everything depends upon the difference between anthropocentric and anthropomorphic, for it is from this difference that we learn how death techniques and life techniques show themselves.

Strictly speaking, the leap from the anthropocentric to the anthropomorphic is but one of a number of possibilities of realizing the turn, and all these paths share the same origin with Heidegger's Holzwege ("country paths"): from the human being to Dasein (existence), from Sprache (language) to Sage (saga, saying), from Gestell (framework) to Ereignis (event, "enownment")." Consequently, the postmodern turn in Feng Shui practices must also entail a turn away from ancient models of anthropocentricism toward contemporary anthropomorphic life techniques, or to quote Schirmacher once again: "Whoever seeks not to dominate humans and nature, but to understand and acknowledge them as existing in a relation to oneself, helps to bring about the disappearance of the conflict." This sums up the idea of living the divine-life or the 'good life' — or of *divination as the idea of just living* — acknowledging our artificial nature as a reservoir of mutual reciprocity that brings into unconcealment auto-poetic forms of existence. Wolfgang Schirmacher, "Technoculture and Life Technique: On the Practice of Hyperperception" http://www.egs.edu/faculty/wolfgang-schirmacher/articles/technoculture-and-life-technique/ (accessed August 2010, 3:43pm) 2, 2.

147 As Wolfgang Schirmacher has noted, when we learn to engage with the "phenomenology of lived ethics" as a practice that is not "norm-oriented" but opens onto the free play of human faculties, then the techne of discipline can come into the open as a poetic means that requires no "authority", and which establishes an "ethos" that "creative openness makes possible." Wolfgang Schirmacher, "Ethics and Artificiality." *Just Living: Philosophy in Artificial Life* (New York: Atropos).

148 "In China, a long-standing policy aimed at restraining the societal position of geomancers and their trade was temporarily reversed when an imperial edict in 1781

legalized fengshui when specifically turned against foreigners. Although sources are scarce, we may assume that this move coincided with anti-foreign and national sentiments of the time, so that fengshui practiced in areas with intensified cultural contact in the late nineteenth century is likely to have acquired a somewhat different character than was the case earlier that century: while it previously contained a metaphoric idiom that mediated social competition between individuals and local areas, it became infused with nationalist discourse to be used as a weapon in the Chinese struggle against western colonial powers... Both the new Republic of 1911 and the Communist state after 1949 fought fengshui beliefs, through an entire century unanimously classified as superstition. Particularly the latter regime has adopted a harsh persecution of practitioners during several campaigns. As a consequence, during the twentieth century the fengshui tradition was under pressure, effecting it to be either played out in a narrowly local and usually private context, mainly in rural areas, or perhaps in some instances to be turned against the Communist state." Ibid. Bruun, *Fengshui in China*, 242-243.

149 "Forms of divination, which in theory and practice had much in common with feng Shui, date back to the earliest Chinese historical records. In the early literature, however, they are referred to as *zhanbu, xiangzhai, kanyu,* (Heaven and Earth), *yin-yang* and *dili* (earth principle/geography), while the term 'feng shui' only became common during the Song Dynasty (96-1279)." Ibid. Brunn, *An Introduction to Feng Shui*, 11.

150 Ibid. 149.

151 Giorgio Agamben, *Profanations* (New York: Zone Books, 2007) 73, 76, 75.

152 Ibid. 77.

153 Ibid. 85.

154 Ibid. 86.

155 Ibid. Bruun, *Fengshui in China*, 256, 257, 260.

156 Perversely, with the advent of Fiberopticism we can invert the infamous pronouncement of Nietzsche's madman, '"Whither is God?"... I will tell you. We have killed him — you and I. All of us are his murders. But how did we do this?"', to 'Of course these tombs and sepulchers have no power within! You and I have invented God once again! How have we resurrected him — we have given him a life without and within! A power of examination based on every whim! Alas, and quite regrettably, we have done it to ourselves — again.' Friedrich Nietzsche, *The Gay Science* (New York: Vintage Books, 1974) 181.

157 Heidegger always speaks of "enframing" as the "supreme danger" of technological appropriation, i.e., of man posited as "standing reserve", of man as "lord of the earth", and of "man everywhere and always only encountering himself" — man as the *anthropocentric object par excellence*. Of course, Fiberopticism adds a very literal twist to the metaphoric premise of technological enframing by threatening to enter the bodily 'frame of man', (nano-technology, electro-discipline, etc.). Martin Heidegger, "The Question Concerning Technology", *Martin Heidegger: Basic Writings: Revised & Expanded Edition*. ed. David Farrel Krell (New York: Harper Collins Publishers, 1993) 332, 332, 332, 332, 332.

158 Wolfgang Schirmacher, "The End of Metaphysics — What Does This Mean?" Social Science Information 23, volume 3 (1984) 603-609.

159 Ibid.

160 Ibid. Agamben, *Profanations*, 83.

161 Ibid. 92.

162 "The coming being is whatever being. In the Scholastic enumeration of transcendentals (*quodlibet ens est unum, verum, bonum seu perfectum* — whatever entity is one, true,

good, or perfect), the term that, remaining unthought in each, conditions the meaning of all the others is the adjective *quodlibet*. The common translation of this term as 'whatever' in the sense of 'it does not matter which, indifferently' is certainly correct, but in its form the Latin says exactly the opposite: *Quodlibet ens* is not "being, it does not matter which," but rather "being such that it always matters." The Latin always already contains, that is, a reference to the will (*libet*). Whatever being has an original relation to desire.

The whatever in question here relates to singularity not in its indifference with respect to a common property (to a concept, for example: being red, being French, being Muslim), but only in its being *such as it is*. Singularity is thus freed from the false dilemma that obliges knowledge to choose between the ineffability of the individual and the intelligibility of the universal. The intelligible, according to a beautiful expression of Levi ben Gershon (Gersonides), is neither a universal nor an individual included in a series, but rather 'singularity insofar as it is whatever singularity'. In this conception, such-and-such being is reclaimed from its having this or that property, which identifies it as belonging to this or that set, to this or that class (the reds, the French, the Muslims) — and it is reclaimed not for another class nor for the simple generic absence of any belonging, but for its being-*such*, for belonging itself. Thus being-*such*, remains constantly hidden in the condition of belonging ('there is an *x such that* it belongs to y') and which is in no way a real predicate, comes to light itself: The singularity exposed as such is whatever you *want*, that is, lovable... Thus, whatever singularity (the Lovable) is never the intelligence of some thing, of this or that quality or essence, but only the intelligence of an intelligibility. Giorgio Agamben, *The Coming Community* (Minneapolis: University of Minnesota Press, 2007) 1-2.

Bibliography

Adams, Matthew. *Self and Social Change.* London: Sage Publishers Ltd., 2007.

Adorno, Theodor W. Adorno & Horkheimer, Max. *Dialectic of Enlightenment: Philosophical Fragments.* Stanford: Stanford University Press, 2002.

Agamben, Giorgio. *Nudities.* Stanford: Stanford University Press, 2011.

_*Profanations.* New York: Zone Books, 2007.

_*The Coming Community.* Minneapolis: University of Minnesota Press, 2007.

_*State of Exception.* Chicago: University of Chicago Press, 2005.

_*Means Without End: Notes on Politics.* Minneapolis: University of Minnesota Press, 2000.

_*Potentialities: Collected Essays in Philosophy.* Stanford: Stanford University Press, 1999.

_*Homo Sacer: Sovereign Power and Bare Life.* Stanford: Stanford University Press, 1998.

_*The Man Without Content.* Stanford: Stanford University Press, 1994.

_*Infancy and History: On the Destruction of Experience.* New York: Verso, 1993.

_*Language and Death: The Place of Negativity.* Minneapolis: University of Minnesota Press, 1991.

Arrigo, Bruce A. and Milovanovic, Dragan. *Revolution in Penology: Rethinking the Society of Captives.* Maryland: Rowman & Littlefield Publishers, Inc. 2009.

Badiou, Alain. *Logics of the Worlds: Being and Event II.* New York: Continuum, 2009.

_*Theory of the Subject.* New York: Continuum, 2009.

_*Conditions.* New York: Continuum, 2008.

_*The Century.* Cambridge: Polity Press, 2007.

_Metapolitics. New York: Verso, 2005.

_Being and Event. New York: Continuum, 2005.

_Theoretical Writings. New York: Continuum, 2004.

_ Infinite Thought: Truth and the return of philosophy. New York: Continuum, 2003.

_Ethics. New York: Verso, 2001.

Ball, Kristie. "Organization, surveillance and the body: toward a politics of resistance." In Theorizing Surveillance: The Panopticon and Beyond, ed. Lyon, David. pgs. 296-317. Portland: Willan Publishing, 2006.

Baudrillard, Jean, Passwords. New York: Verso, 2003.

_Simulacra and Simulation. Ann Arbor: The University of Michigan Press, 2003.

_Screened Out. New York: Verso, 2002.

_Impossible Exchange. New York: Verso, 2001.

_The Perfect Crime. New York: Verso, 1996.

_The System of Objects. New York: Verso, 1996.

_The Transparency of Evil: Essays on Extreme Phenomena. New York: Verso, 1993.

_ Seduction. New York: St. Martin's Press, 1990.

_The Ecstasy of Communication. New York: Semiotext(e), 1988.

_Forget Foucault. New York: Semiotext(e), 1987.

_Simulations. New York: Semiotext(e), 1983.

_In the Shadow of Silent Majorities. New York: Semiotext(e), 1983.

_The Mirror of Production. Saint Louis: Telos Press, 1975.

Bauman, Zygmunt. Liquid Times: Living in an Age of Uncertainty. Cambridge: Polity Press, 2007.

_Liquid Fear. Cambridge: Polity Press, 2006.

_Liquid Life. Cambridge: Polity Press, 2005.

_Liquid Love. Cambridge: Polity Press, 2003.

_Liquid Modernity. Cambridge: Polity Press, 2000.

Beck, John C. and Davenport, Thomas H. The Attention Economy: Understanding the New Currency of Business. Boston: Harvard

Business School Press, 2001.

Beckett, Katherine & Herbert, Steve. *Banished: The New Social Control in Urban America* (Studies in Crime and Public Policy). New York: Oxford University Press, 2010.

Beirne, Piers. *Inventing Criminology: Essays in the Rise of 'Homo Criminalis'* (SUNY Series in Deviance and Social Control). New York: State University of New York Press, 1993.

Beller, Jonathan. *The cinematic mode of production: Attention economy and the society of spectacle.* Hanover: University Press of New England, 2006.

Benjamin, Walter. *The Origin of the German Tragic Drama.* New York: Verso, 1998.

_Selected Writings: Volume I, 1913-1926. Massachusetts: The Belknap Press of Harvard University Press, 1996.

_*Benjamin: Philosophy, Aesthetics.* History. ed. Gary Smith. Chicago: University of Chicago Press, 1983.

_*Illuminations: Essays and Reflections.* New York: Schocken books, 1968.

Benko, Georges and Strohmayer, Ulf. ed. *Space and Social Theory: Interpreting Modernity and Postmodernity.* Malden: Blackwell Publishers Inc., 1997.

Bentham, Jeremy. *The Rationale of Punishment.* New York: Prometheus Books, 2009.

Bell, Daniel. *The Cultural Contradictions of Capitalism.* New York: Basic Books, 1976.

_*The Coming of Post-Industrial Society.* New York: Basic Books, 1999.

Berardi, Franco 'Bifo'. *The Soul at Work: From Alienation to Autonomy.* Los Angeles: Semiotext(e), 2009.

Bergman, Gregory & Archer, Peter. *I watch therefore I am.* Avon: Adams Media, 2011.

Bigo, Didier, "Globalized (in)security: the field and the ban-optic." In *Terror, Insecurity and Liberty: Illiberal practices of liberal regimes after 9/11.* ed. Bigo, Didier & Tsoukala, Anastassia. pgs

10-48. New York: Routledge, 2008.

Bigo, Didier & Tsoukala, Anastassia, ed. *Terror, Insecurity and Liberty: Illiberal practices of liberal regimes after 9/11*. New York: Routledge, 2008.

Bogard, William, *The Simulation of Surveillance: Hypercontrol in telematic societies*. New York: Cambridge University Press, 1996.

Brown, Simon. *Principles of Feng Shui*. London: Thorsons, 1996.

Bruun, Ole. *Fengshui in China: Geomantic Divination Between State Orthodoxy and Popular Religion*. Honolulu: University of Hawai'i Press, 2003.

_ *An Introduction to Feng Shui*. New York: Cambridge University Press, 2008.

Butler, Judith. *Frames of War: When Is Life Grievable?* New York: Verso, 2009.

_*Giving an Account of Oneself*. New York: Fordham Press, 2005
_*Precarious Life: The Powers of Mourning and Violence*. New York: Verso, 2004.

_*The Psychic Life of Power: Theories in Subjection*. Stanford: Stanford University Press, 1997.

Casey, Edward S. *The Fate of Place: A Philosophical History*. Los Angeles: University of California Press, 1998.

Castel, Helen, ed. *Folding in Architecture*. Great Britain: Wiley-Academy, 2004.

Chriss, James. *Social Control: An Introduction*. Malden: Polity Press, 2007.

Colker, Ruth. *American Law in the Age of Hypercapitalism: The Worker, The Family, The State*. New York: New York University Press, 1998.

Crampton, Jeremy W., and Elden, Stuart, ed. *Space, Knowledge and Power: Foucault and Geography*. Burlington: Ashgate Publishing Limited, 2010.

De Angelis, Massimo. *The Beginning of History: Value Struggles and Global Capital*. London: Pluto Press, 2007.

Debord, Guy. *A Sick Planet*. New York: Seagull books, 2004.

_*Comments on the Society of Spectacle*. New York: Verso, 1998.

_*The Society of Spectacle*. New York: Zone Books, 1995.

De Certeau, Michel. *The Practice of Everyday Life*. Los Angles: University of California Press, 1984.

Dehaene, Michiel, and De Cauter, Lieven., ed. *Heterotopia and the City: Public space in postcivil society*. New York: Routledge, 2008.

Deleuze, Gilles. *Two Regimes of Madness*. Los Angeles: Semiotext(e), 2006.

_*The Fold: Leibniz and the Baroque*. Minneapolis: University of Minnesota Press, 1993.

_*Foucault*, Minneapolis: University of Minnesota Press, 1986.

Deleuze, Gilles, and Guattari, Felix. *A Thousand Plateaus: Capitalism and Schizophrenia*. Minneapolis: University of Minnesota Press, 1987.

_Anti-Oedipus: Capitalism and Schizophrenia. Minneapolis: University of Minnesota Press, 1983.

Derrida, Jacques. *Specters of Marx: The State of Debt, the Work of Mourning & the New International*. New York: Routledge, 1994.

_*Given Time I. Counterfeit Money*. Chicago: Chicago University Press 1992.

Draffan, George & Jensen Derrick. *Welcome to the Machine: Science, Surveillance and the Culture of Control*. Vermont: Chelsea Green Publishing, 2004.

Elden, Stuart. *Mapping the Present: Heidegger, Foucault and the Project of a Spatial History*. New York: Continuum, 2001.

Ernest J. Eitel. *What is Feng-Shui? The Classic Nineteenth Century Interpretation*. New York: Dover Publications Inc., 2003.

Feuchtwang, Stephan. *An Anthropology of Analysis of Chinese Geomancy*. Vientiane: Vitagna, 1974.

Florida, Richard. *The Flight of the Creative Class: The New Global Competition for Talent*. New York: Harper Business, 2005.

_*The Rise of the Creative Class... and how it's transforming work,* *leisure, community & everyday life*. New York: Basic Books, 2002.

Foucault, Michel. *History of Madness*. New York: Routledge, 2006.

_*The Birth of Biopolitics, Lectures as the Collège de France: 1978-1979*. ed. Senellart, Michel. New York: Palgrave/MacMillan, 2008.

_*Fearless Speech*. Los Angeles: Semiotext(e), 2001.

_ *Religion and culture*. ed. Carrette, Jeremy R. New York: Routledge, 1999.

_*Aesthetics, Method, and Epistemology*. Ed. Faubion, James D. New York: The New Press, 1998.

_ *Remarks on Marx*. New York: Semiotext(e), 1991.

_*The Use of Pleasure: Volume II of the History of Sexuality*. New York: Vintage Books, 1990.

_ *The History of Sexuality, An Introduction: Volume I*. New York: Vintage Books, 1990.

_*Mental Illness and Psychology*. Los Angeles: University of California Press, 1987.

_*The Care of the Self, The History of Sexuality: Volume III*, New York: Vintage Books, 1986.

_*Politics, Philosophy, Culture: Interviews and Other Writings 1977-1984*. Ed. Kritzman, Lawrence D. New York: Routledge, 1988.

_*Power/Knowledge: Selected Interviews & Other Writings, 1972-1977*. Ed. Gordon, Colin. New York: Pantheon Books, 1980.

_*Discipline and Punish: The Birth of the Prison*. New York: Vintage Books, 1977.

_*Language, Counter-memory, Practice: Selected essays and interviews by Michel Foucault*. New York: Cornell University Press, 1977.

_*The Archeology of Knowledge & The Discourse on Language*. New York: Pantheon Books, 1972.

_*The Order of Things: An Archaeology of the Human Sciences*. New York: Vintage Books, 1970.

Friedman, Lawrence. *Guarding Life's Dark Secrets: Legal and Social Control over Reputation, Propriety and Privacy.* Stanford: Stanford University Press, 2007.

Gandy Jr., Oscar H. "Quixotics unite! Engaging pragmatists on rational discrimination." In *Theorizing Surveillance: The Panopticon and Beyond.* ed. Lyon, David. Pgs. 318-336. Portland: Willan Publishing, 2006.

Galston, David. *Archives and the Event of God: The Impact of Michel Foucault on Philosophical Theology* (McGill-Queen's Studies in the History of Religion). Canada: McGill-Queen's University Press, 2010.

Garland, David. *The Culture of Social Control: Crime and Social Order in Contemporary Society.* Chicago: The University of Chicago Press, 2001.

Gilmore, James H. and Pine II, Joseph B. *The Experience Economy: Work is Theater & Every Business a Stage.* Boston: Harvard Business School Press, 1999.

_*Markets of One: Creating Customer Unique Value through Mass Customization.* Boston: A Harvard Business Review Book, 2000.

Gates, Hill. *China's Motor: A Thousand Years of Petty Capitalism.* New York: Cornell University Press, 1996.

Gobé, Marc. *Emotional Branding: The New Paradigm for Connecting Brands to People.* New York: Allworth Press, 2009.

Goetz, Stewart, and Taliaferro, Charles. *A Brief History Of The Soul.* Malden: Wiley-Blackwell, 2011.

Gorz, André. *Critique of Economic Reason.* New York: Verso, 1998.

Graham, Phil. *Hypercapitalism: New Media, Language, and Social Perceptions of Value.* New York: Peter Lang Publishing Inc., 2006.

Guattari, Felix. *The Machinic Unconscious: Essays in Schizoanalysis.* Los Angeles: Semiotext(e), 2011.

_*The Anti-Oedipus Papers.* Los Angeles: Semiotext(e), 2006.

_*The Three Ecologies.* New Brunswick: The Athlone Press, 2000.

_*Soft Subversions.* New York: Semiotext(e), 1996.

_Chaosophy. New York: Semiotext(e), 1995.

_Chaosmosis: an ethico-aesthetic paradigm. Indianapolis: Indiana University Press, 1992.

_Molecular Revolutions: Psychiatry and Politics. New York: Penguin Books, 1984.

Haggerty, Kevin D. "Tear down the walls: on demolishing the panopticon." In Theorizing Surveillance: The Panopticon and Beyond. ed. Lyon, David. pgs. 23-45. Portland: Willan Publishing, 2006.

Haraway, Donna J. Simians, Cyborgs, and Women: The Reinvention of Nature. New York: Routledge, 1991.

Hardt, Michael, and Negri, Antonio. Commonwealth. Cambridge: The Belknap Press of Harvard University Press, 2009.

_Multitude: War and Democracy in the Age of Empire. New York: The Penguin Press, 2004.

_Empire. Cambridge: Harvard University Press, 2000.

Harris, Shane. The Watchers: The Rise of America's Surveillance State. New York: Penguin Press, 2010.

Hegel, Georg Wilhelm Friedrich. Lectures on Logic. Indianapolis: Indiana University Press, 2001.

_Reason in History. New Jersey: Prentice-Hall Inc., 1997.

_Introduction to The Philosophy of History. Cambridge: Hackett Publishing, 1988.

_Hegel's Phenomenology of Spirit. Oxford: Oxford University Press, 1977.

Heidegger, Martin. Mindfulness. New York: Continuum, 2006.

_Introduction to Metaphysics. New Haven: Yale University Press, 2000.

_Contributions to Philosophy (From Enknowing). Indianapolis: Indiana University Press, 1999.

_Being and Time. New York: State University of New York Press, 1996.

_Basic Writings: Revised and Expanded Edition, ed. Krell, David Farrell. San Francisco: Harper San Francisco, 1993.

_Poetry, Language, Thought. New York: Perennial Classics, 1971.

Herzfeld, Michael. *The Production of Indifference.* Chicago: University of Chicago Press, 1992.

Illouz, Eva. *Cold Intimacies: The making of Emotional Capitalism.* Cambridge: Polity Press, 2007.

Innes, Martin. *Understanding Social Control: Deviance, Crime and Social Order.* England: Open University Press, 2003.

Fredric Jameson. *A Singular Modernity: Essay on the Ontology of the Present.* New York: Verso, 2002.

_The Cultural Turn: Selected Writings on the Postmodern, 1983-1998. New York: Verso, 1998.

_ Postmodernism or, The Cultural Logic of Late Capitalism. Durham: Duke University Pres, 1991.

_The Political Unconscious: Narrative as a Socially Symbolic Act. New York: Cornell University Press, 1981.

Jencks, Charles. *The New Paradigm in Architecture.* New Haven: Yale University Press, 2002.

_ed. *Deconstruction in Architecture.* New York: St. Martin's Press, 1988.

_What is Postmodernism? West Sussex: Academy Editions, 1986.

Klein, Naomi. *The Shock Doctrine: The Rise of Disaster Capitalism.* New York: Picador, 2007.

Klein, Norman. *Freud in Coney Island and Other Tales.* Los Angeles: Otis books/Seismicity editions, 2006.

_The Vatican to Vegas: A History of Special Effects. New York: The New Press, 2004.

Kroker, Arthur. *The Will to Technology & The Culture of Nihilism.* Toronto: University of Toronto Press, 2004.

_The Possessed Individual: technology and the french postmodern. New York: St. Martin's, 1992.

Kroker, Arthur and Cook, David. *The Postmodern Scene: Excremental Culture and Hyper Aesthetics.* New York: St.

Martin's, 1986.

Kroker, Arthur and Kroker, Marilouise and Cook, David. *Panic Encyclopedia: the definitive guide to the postmodern scene.* New York: St. Martin's Press, 1989.

Lacan, Jacques. *My Teachings.* New York: Verso, 2008.

_*Ecrits: A Selection.* New York: W.W. Norton and Company, 1999.

_*The Four Fundamental Concepts of Psychoanalysis: The Seminar of Jacques Lacan: Book XI.* New York: W&W. Norton and Company, 1998.

_*Freud's Papers on Technique: The Seminar of Jacques Lacan: Book I.* New York: W.W. Norton and Company, 1991.

Leach, Neil. *The Anaethetics of Architecture.* Massachusetts: MIT Press, 1999.

_ed. *Rethinking Architecture: a reader in cultural theory.* New York: Routledge, 1997.

Leibniz, Gottfried Wilhelm. *Philosophical Texts.* ed. Woolhouse, R.S. and Francks, Richard. Oxford: Oxford University Press, 1998.

_*Writings on China.* Illinois, Open Court Publishing, 1994.

Lewis, Mark Edward. *The Construction of Space in Early China.* New York: State University of New York Press, 2006.

Lip, Evelyn. *Chinese Geomancy.* Singapore: Times Books International, 1996.

_*Feng Shui: Environments of Power, A Study of Chinese Architecture.* London: Academy Editions, 1996.

Los, Maria. "Looking into the future: surveillance, globalization and the totalitarian potential." In *Theorizing Surveillance: The Panopticon and Beyond.* ed. Lyon, David. pgs. 69-94. Portland: Willan Publishing, 2006.

Lynn, Greg. "Introduction", In Folding in Architecture, ed. Castel, Helen. pgs. 9-13. Great Britain: Wiley-Academy, 1999.

Lyotard, Jean-Francois. *Libidinal Economy.* Indianapolis: Indiana University Press, 1993.

The Postmodern Explained. Minneapolis: University of Minnesota Press, 1992.

The Differend: Phrases in Dispute (Theory and History of Literature, Volume 46). Minneapolis: University of Minnesota Press, 1988.

_ The Postmodern Condition: A Report on Knowledge._ Minneapolis: University of Minnesota Press, 1984.

Driftworks. New York: Semiotext(e), 1984.

Lyon, David. _The Electronic Eye: The Rise of Surveillance Society._ Minneapolis: University of Minnesota, 1994.

_ ed. _Theorizing Surveillance: The Panopticon and Beyond._ Portland: Willan Publishing, 2009.

_ _Surveillance after September 11._ Cambridge: Polity Press, 2003.

_"An Electronic Panopticon? A Sociological Critique of Surveillance Theory", Sociological Review 41 (4), pgs. 653-678. New York: Wiley-Blackwell, 1993.

Marazzi, Christian. _The Violence of Financial Capitalism._ Los Angeles: Semiotext(e), 2010.

Capital and Language: From the New Economy to the War Economy. Los Angeles: Semiotext(e), 2007.

The Violence of Financial Capitalism. Los Angeles: Semiotext(e), 2010.

Marsden, Richard. _The Nature of Capital: Marx after Foucault._ New York: Routledge, 1999.

Martin, Raymond, and Barresi, John. _The Rise and Fall of Soul and Self: An Intellectual History of Personal Identity._ New York: Columbia University Press, 2006.

Mathiesen, Thomas. "The Viewer Society: Michel Foucault's Panopticon Revisited." In Theoretical Criminology 1 (2). Pgs 215-234. New York: Sage Publishing, May, 1997.

Marx, Karl. _The Communist Manifesto._ New York: Verso, 1998.

The 18th of Brumaire of Louis of Bonaparte. New York: International Publishers, 1998.

The German Ideology. New York: Prometheus Book, 1998.

_The Poverty of Philosophy. New York: Prometheus Books, 1995.

_Grundrisse. New York: Penguin books, 1993.

_Capital Volume II. New York: Penguin Books, 1992.

_Capital Volume III. New York: Penguin Books, 1991.

_Economic and Philosophic Manuscripts of 1844. New York: Prometheus books, 1988.

_Capital Volume I. New York: Penguin Books, 1976.

_A Contribution to the Critique of Political Economy. New York: International Publishers, 1970.

Mészáros, István. The Structural Crisis of Capital. New York: The Monthly Review Press, 2010.

McGushin, Edward F. Foucault's Askesis: An Introduction to the Philosophical Life. Evanston: Northwestern University Press, 2007.

Mehta, Michael D. "On Nano-Panopticism: A Sociological Perspective." http://chem4823.usask.ca/cassidyr/OnNano-Panopticism-ASociologicalPerspective.htm, accessed August 15th, 2011, 1:13pm.

Miller, Jacques-Alain. "Jeremy Bentham's Panoptic Device", October 41, summer. Cambridge: MIT Press, 1987.

Monahan, Prof. Torin. Surveillance in the Time of Insecurity (Critical Issues in Crime and Society). New Brunswick: Rutgers University Press, 2010.

Murakami, David Wood. "Beyond the Panopticon: Foucault and Surveillance Studies." In Space, Knowledge and Power: Foucault and Geography. ed. Crampton, Jeremy W. & Elden, Stuart. pgs. 245-264. Burlington: Ashgate Publishing Limited, 2010.

Nealon, Jeffery T. Foucault Beyond Foucault: Power and its Intensifications since 1984. Stanford: Stanford University Press, 2008.

Negri, Antonio. The Porcelain Workshop: For a New Grammar of Politics. Los Angeles: Semiotext(e), 2008.

_The Politics of Subversion: A Manifesto for the Twenty-First

Century. Cambridge: Polity Press, 2005.

_*Time for Revolution.* New York: Continuum, 2003.

Nietzsche, Friedrich. *Thus Spoke Zarathrustra.* Oxford: Oxford University Press, 2005.

_*Daybreak: Thoughts on the Prejudices of Morality.* Cambridge: Cambridge University Press, 1997.

_*Untimely Meditations.* Cambridge: Cambridge University Press, 1997.

_*Beyond Good and Evil.* New York: Vintage Books, 1989.

_*Human, All Too Human: A Book for Free Spirits.* Cambridge: Cambridge University Press, 1986.

_*The Gay Science.* New York: Vintage books, 1974.

_*The Will to Power.* New York: Vintage Books, 1968.

North, Douglass C. & Wallis, John Joseph & Weingast, Barry R. *Violence and Social Orders: A Conceptual Framework for Interpreting Recorded Human History.* New York: Cambridge University Press, 2009.

Ogura, Toshimaru. "Electronic government and surveillance oriented society." In *Theorizing Surveillance: The Panopticon and Beyond.* ed. Lyon, David. pgs. 270-295. Portland: Willan Publishing, 2006.

Ouellet, Maxime. "Cybernetic capitalism and the global information society." In *Cultural Political Economy.* ed., Best, Jacqueline & Paterson, Matthew. pgs. 177-186. New York: Routledge, 2010.

Papadakis, Dr. Anreas C. *Deconstruction III,* London: Academy Group ltd., 1990.

_*Deconstruction II,* London: Academy Group ltd., 1989.

_*Deconstruction / Reconstruction,* London: Academy Group ltd., 1989.

Paras, Eric, *Foucault 2.0: Beyond Power and Knowledge.* New York: Other Press, 2006.

Pine II, B. Joseph. *Mass Customization: The New Frontier in Business Competition.* Boston: Harvard Business School Press, 1993.

Postman, Neil. *The Disappearance of Childhood.* New York: Vintage books, 1994.

_*Technopoly: The Surrender of Culture to Technology.* New York: Vintage Books, 1993.

_*Amusing Ourselves to Death.* New York: Penguin books, 1985.

Poster, Mark. *Foucault, Marxism & History: Mode of Production versus Mode of Information.* Cambridge: Polity Press, 1984.

_ *The Mode of Information: Poststructuralism and Social Context.* Cambridge: Polity Press, 1990.

Reich, Robert B. *Supercapitalism: The Transformation of Business, Democracy, and Everyday Life.* New York: Alfred A. Knopf, 2007.

Rescher, Nicholas. *On Leibniz.* Pittsburg: University of Pittsburg Press, 2003.

_ *G.W. Liebniz's Monodalology.* Pittsburg: Pittsburg University Press, 1991.

Rifkin, Jeremy. *The Age of Access: The New Culture of Hypercapitalism where all of life is a paid-for experience.* New York: Jeremy P. Tarcher/ Putnam, 2001.

Reynolds, Bryan. *Transversal Subjects: From Montaigne to Deleuze after Derrida.* New York: Palgrave MacMillian, 2009.

Schirmacher, Wolfgang. "Technoculture and Life Technique: On the Practice of Hyperperception." http://www.egs.edu/ faculty/wolfgang-schirmacher/articles/technoculture-and-life-technique/, accessed August 2010, 3:43pm.

_"Ethics and Artificiality". In *Wolfgang Schirmacher, Just Living: Philosophy in Artificial Life.* New York: Atropos.

_"Privacy as an Ethical Problem in the Computer Society". Philosophy and Technology II. (Boston Studies in the Philosophy of Science 90) ed. C, Mitcham. Reidel: Dordrecht, 1986.

_"The End of Metaphysics – What Does This Mean?", In *Social Science Information* 23, volume 3, pgs. 603-309. New York: Sage Publishing, 1984.

Schmitt, Bernd H. *Experiential Marketing: How to get customers to sense, fee, think, act (and) relate to your company and brands*. New York: The Free Press, 1999.

Schmitt, Carl. *The Concept of the Political*. Chicago: Chicago University Press, 2007.

_*Theory of the Partisan*. New York: Telos Press Publishing, 2007.

_*Political Theology: Four Chapters on the Concept of Sovereignty*. Chicago: Chicago University Press, 2005.

_*The Nomos of the Earth: in the International Law of Jus Publicum Europaeum*. New York: Telos Press Publishing, 2003.

Sennett, Richard. *The Culture of the New Capitalism*. New Haven: Yale University Press, 2006.

Skinner, Stephen. *Terrestrial Astrology: Divination by Geomancy*. London: Routledge, 1980.

Smith, Philip. *Punishment and Culture*. Chicago: University of Chicago Press, 2008.

Smith, Richard J. *Fortune-tellers and Philosophers: Divination in Chinese Society*. Boulder: Westview Press, 1991.

Sprinker, Michael. ed. *Ghostly Demarcations: A Symposium on Jacques Derrida's Specters of Marx*. New York: Verso, 1999.

Venturi, Robert. *Complexity and Contradiction in Architecture*. New York: The Museum of Modern Art, 1966.

Paul Virilio, *The University of Disaster*. Cambridge: Polity Press, 2010.

_*Negative Horizon*. New York: Continuum, 2005.

_*The Original Accident*. Cambridge: Polity Press, 2005.

_*Crepuscular Dawn*. Los Angeles: Semiotext(e), 2002.

_*The Information Bomb*. New York: Verso, 200.

_*Polar Inertia*. Thousand Oaks: Sage Publishing, 2000.

_*Open Sky*. New York: Verso, 1997.

_*The Aesthetics of Disappearance*. New York: Semiotext(e), 1991.

_*Speed & Politics*. New York: Semiotext(e), 1986.

_*Pure War*. New York: Semiotext(e), 1983.

Zbikowski, Dörte. "The Listening Era: The Phenomena of

Acoustic Surveillance." In *CRTL SPACE: Rhetorics of Surveillance from Bentham to Big Brother*. ed. Levin, Thomas & Frohne, Ursula & Weibel, Peter. pgs. 32-49. Massachusetts: MIT Press, 2002.

Zielinski, Siegfried. *Deep Time of the Media: Toward an Archeology of Hearing and Seeing by Technological Means*. Cambridge: MIT Press, 2006.

_*Audiovisions: Cinema and television as entr'actes in history*. Amsterdam: Amsterdam University Press, 1999.

Zetter, Kim. "Anonymous Hacks Security Firm Investigating It: Releases E-mail." *Wired* http://www.wired.com/threatlevel /2011/02/anonymous-hacks-hbgary/, accessed Feb 5th, 2011, 5:50pm.

Zizek, Slavoj. *Living in the End Times*. New York: Verso, 2010.

_*First as Tragedy, Then as Farce*. New York: Verso, 2009.

_ *Violence*. New York: Picador, 2008.

_*The Parallax View*. Massachusetts: MIT Press, 2008.

_*In Defense of Lost Causes*. New York: Verso, 2008.

_ *Organs without Bodies: On Deleuze and Consequences*. New York: Routledge, 2004.

_*For they know not what they do: Enjoyment as a political factor*. New York: Verso, 1991.

_*The Sublime Object of Ideology*. New York: Verso, 1989.

Contemporary culture has eliminated both the concept of the public and the figure of the intellectual. Former public spaces – both physical and cultural – are now either derelict or colonized by advertising. A cretinous anti-intellectualism presides, cheerled by expensively educated hacks in the pay of multinational corporations who reassure their bored readers that there is no need to rouse themselves from their interpassive stupor. The informal censorship internalized and propagated by the cultural workers of late capitalism generates a banal conformity that the propaganda chiefs of Stalinism could only ever have dreamt of imposing. Zer0 Books knows that another kind of discourse – intellectual without being academic, popular without being populist – is not only possible: it is already flourishing, in the regions beyond the striplit malls of so-called mass media and the neurotically bureaucratic halls of the academy. Zer0 is committed to the idea of publishing as a making public of the intellectual. It is convinced that in the unthinking, blandly consensual culture in which we live, critical and engaged theoretical reflection is more important than ever before.